THE HUMANITIES IN THE WORLD

The Humanities in the World

Edited by
Anders Engberg-Pedersen

The Humanities in the World
Edited by Anders Engberg-Pedersen

© Anders Engberg-Pedersen and U Press 2020

Graphic design and cover: Ordered by Colour
Printed by Specialtrykkeriet Arco
Printed in Denmark 2020
ISBN: 978-87-93060-98-2

No part of this book may be reproduced, stored
in a retrieval system, or transmitted in any form
or by any means, including mechanical, electronic,
photocopying, recording, or otherwise, without the
prior written permission of the publisher.

U PRESS
Rådhuspladsen 16
DK-1550 Copenhagen
www.upress.dk

Published with the financial support of
the Carlsberg Foundation

CONTENT

7 Introduction
The Humanities in the World
Anders Engberg-Pedersen, Mikkel Bille,
Karen Gram-Skjoldager

24 On Not "Justifying" the Humanities
Stefan Collini

54 The Humanities beyond Interpretation
Onora O'Neill

79 How the Humanities Have Changed the World
Rens Bod

Introduction
The Humanities in the World

Anders Engberg-Pedersen, Mikkel Bille,
Karen Gram-Skjoldager

When the Indian linguist Panini developed a grammar for Sanskrit in around 500 BCE, he probably did not envision that some 2500 years later his discovery would be used to develop algorithms in computers. But in 1959, when the computer scientist John Backus designed the syntax for ALGOL60 – the first high-level programming language – he based it on Panini's grammar. Panini had discovered a set of rules, and a method of applying them, which allowed for a description of the infinite number of sentences in Sanskrit with a finite number of rules and applications. For Backus, this ancient discovery in linguistics had implications for the emergent field of information technology. The sequential application of rules to arrive at a linguistic utterance could serve as a template for a different kind of language – computer algorithms. And thus, the first of numerous high-level programming languages saw the light of day.[1]

The use of an ancient grammar in the development of modern information technology – a development which has since transformed the lifeworld of most people on the planet – is one of the more direct examples of the worldliness of humanistic knowledge. Few discoveries and inventions in the humanities lead to direct applications of this sort. But the work conducted in the humanities is not only firmly located in and shaped by the world, it is also strongly engaged with the world, and has a profound impact on it. Aside from obvious places such as museums, art galleries, and schools, we may point to the importance of archaeological, anthropological, and historical expertise in investigations of war and genocides. Here methods of excavation and bone analysis – often drawing heavily on the natural sciences – and humanistic interpretative skills have played a key role in forensic investigations. Indeed, such is the power of humanities insights and perspectives that even the commercial sector has increasingly sought to adopt them. The success of companies such as Apple is often partly attributed to fruitful collaboration between the liberal arts and technology, focusing on human perception and lifeworlds to develop technologies that make sense in everyday life. Likewise, consultancy companies such as ReD Associates, which services major companies like Lego, Adidas, and Ford, employ humanities graduates from top universities and use their critical skills to understand human sensemaking. This particular company explicitly promotes phenomenology and lack of hypothesis as their starting point when shaping new businesses and technologies.

Most often, however, insights from the humanities develop and shape the ideas that circulate throughout society. New concepts and careful analyses help individuals navigate the challenges and concerns that preoccupy us at any given time. How, for example, should we think about belonging, communities, borders, and privacy in an era of climate change, mass migration, unending war, and digital surveillance? The historical frames, analytical vocabularies, and newly minted concepts of humanities scholarship have much to offer in this regard. But even if the impact of the human sciences is widespread, it can be difficult to measure. The worldliness of the humanities is often hidden, neglected, or simply forgotten. Indeed, talk of 'the humanities' today almost immediately generates a vocabulary of crisis. Programmes and departments are cut, humanistic inquiry is decried as an insignificant yet expensive luxury, and student numbers are dropping. From 2012 to 2017 the number of bachelor's degrees in the humanities conferred in the US went down by 10%, and in 2017 the proportion of students doing a humanities degree fell below 12% of all degrees awarded for the first time since data became available.[2] As a consequence, a series of defences of the humanities have appeared in recent years. Though well-intentioned, these defences have often adopted an apologetic tone and have sought succour in more abstract values, stressing the role of the humanities in the formation of *Bildung* or 'self-cultivation', in the development of democratic competences, and in the practice of critical thinking. Such grand claims about the unique purpose and power of the humanities risk substituting one myth with another. If the ivory tower was once a positive metaphor to signify the required isolation from the mundane pressures and exigencies that distract from the pursuit of systematic knowledge, as in the Humboldt tradition, then it has since developed into a moniker that signifies the perceived irrelevance and isolationism of the humanities. In attempting to debunk this myth of the ivory tower, however, defences of the sort mentioned above are in danger of establishing an equally mythological belief: that the unique mission of the humanities is, ultimately, to save the world. This particular public projection of the field is not without its problems. For one, it sits uncomfortably with the increased specialization, introversion, and striving for excellence that characterizes much humanities research today. Likewise, and perhaps more problematically, it often builds on implicit or explicit assumptions about the moral and political superiority of the discipline that may in fact hamper engagement with and support for it.

This short book adopts a different approach. Charting the territory between the two extremes, it argues for and exemplifies an at once more modest and more constructive perspective that highlights the worldliness of the humanities. Instead of locating the value and force of the humanities in general values and competences, it argues for a more concrete and practical perspective by bringing to light how various humanistic fields have long been and continue to be entangled with the wider scientific and social world. Beneath the lofty claims that department heads, deans, and university presidents like to make about the mission and ultimate purpose of humanistic inquiry, humanist scholars are engaged in much more mundane activities that often fly under the radar in discussion of the humanities. We need a better account of what the humanities are, what humanist scholars do and how they do it, what is done with the knowledge they produce, and how this knowledge seeps into society and other institutions and sciences through multiple channels to shape our common world. For example, a recent study has shown that within the past three years, 90% of Danish humanities researchers have been involved in activities that include partners outside universities.[3] But what is it exactly that humanities researchers do when they 'do' humanities research, and how should we speak about the humanities today, in all its diversity, from archaeology, literature, and languages, to film studies, pedagogy, and philosophy? What is the nature of humanistic inquiry? And how have the humanities changed the world? Answers to these questions require exploration from different perspectives. This book presents three such perspectives. It comprises three essays that take a social-political, a philosophical, and an historical point of view to articulate and even rethink the nature and practice of humanities research.

How to speak of the humanities

To speak of the 'humanities' is to speak of an idea and a group of disciplines whose collective unity only emerged fairly recently. The 'humanities' arose as a concept in the US in the middle of the twentieth century as a reaction against an aggressive positivism in the 1930s and 1940s that denigrated all forms of knowledge that did not conform to the methods of the natural sciences. As a counterpoint, the systematic inquiries into history, language, literature, and the arts were gathered under the heading of 'the humanities'.[4] The conceptual and institutional separation of these subjects from other modes of scientific inquiry, however, is the result of a longer historical trajectory. Even in the process of scientific differentiation that took place during the nineteenth century, the human sciences appear as a distinct realm of inquiry whose unique charge was the interpretation of the manifestations of human expression as opposed to – and often in competition with – the natural sciences and their efforts to explain the natural world. Thus, in his introduction to the human sciences or *Geisteswissenschaften*, Wilhelm Dilthey made the famous distinction between *verstehen* (understanding) and *erklären* (explaining) that has shaped the general conception of both the purpose and the methods of the humanities and the natural sciences ever since.[5]

A corollary of this division is the assumed perception of the contributions the two fields make to society. The knowledge output of the natural sciences is often turned into patents and technological inventions that in turn generate business and jobs and lead to visible and measurable changes in our everyday lives. On the other hand, the humanities, we hear, have little real-world impact. Interpretation – historical, literary, cultural, or otherwise – does not only not lead to patents and economic growth, it is irrelevant to matters of import and hardly leaves any mark on our society.

One of the established defences of the humanities willingly accepts this line of thinking. Knowing about the emergence of Ancient Greek democracy, the representation of gender in Hamlet, or tribal culture and language in Indonesia is valuable in and of itself. Willfully ignoring concerns about measurable consequences or impact, the humanities are 'intrinsically valuable', as the phrase goes. We do not need to transform or translate one value into another, be it economic or practical, for it to be meaningful and worth our time. According to this line of thinking, as Helen Small writes, the value of the humanities is "wrapped up in objects and activities, which could be deemed… self-justifying".[6] And indeed, much work done in the humanities is distinctly non-utilitarian in nature – its aim is 'only' the pursuit of knowledge and the use of this knowledge to enlighten and enrich the populations that together constitute our civil societies. Just like many questions in the natural sciences (When was the Big Bang? How large is the universe?), knowledge is an end in itself.

But proclaiming this important role of the humanities as their prime or sole purpose is not always helpful. It conjures a concept of the humanities as an isolated, self-sufficient field of scholarship cordoned off both from the activities in the other sciences and from society. And it disregards entirely the often invisible, but very concrete impact humanities scholarship has on the world. To bring this to light we may begin by rethinking the concept of 'the humanities' itself. Gathering the multiple activities, purposes, and worldly engagements related to goals as distinct as the detailed analysis of a visual image in its social and political context, the organizing of a large corpus of linguistic utterances, or the development of normative claims about the ethics of punishment in the singular collective 'THE humanities' erases the concrete activities of each field and inevitably leads to abstraction. Speaking of visual culture, linguistics, and philosophy in this abstract way very quickly produces yet further abstractions and the noble but somewhat intangible defences touting *Bildung*, democratic competences, and critical thinking mentioned above.

In the first chapter of this book, 'On Not "Justifying" the Humanities' Stefan Collini points out that we would do well to go in the opposite direction – toward the specific and the concrete. This entails developing a set of clear descriptions of what humanists actually do, of the problems they grapple with and their means for solving them, and how their findings are disseminated. Descending one or more levels of abstraction, from 'the humanities' to, for example, musicology or history, and from history to historians of the Middle East, and from there to their specific topics and methods, will make visible the everyday, worldly engagement of humanities scholarship. Such descriptions may signal much more clearly to politicians, funding bodies, and the wider public what humanist scholars actually do, as well as showing the very real problems that they try to tackle. Once we leave the airy realms of abstraction, we might begin to see the wealth of activities, exchanges, debates, and collaborations between the social world and the work carried out by humanist scholars of various stripes. In other words, if we do not want to short-change the field and ignore a major and significant part of its activities, we need to learn how to speak of the humanities.

There are good historical reasons for our inability to speak concretely of the humanities. Universities have long been comparably small institutions for the select few who overwhelmingly hail from the privileged segments of society. Laying claim to relatively few economic means, scholars in the humanities were not pushed to justify themselves or their work. But as Collini points out in his essay, the socio-political conditions have markedly changed the university as an institution in the twentieth and twenty-first centuries. With the vast expansion of higher education in Europe and the US after 1945, the university has been transformed from an elite to a mass institution, while the ideology that underpinned the expansion of education in many European countries has in the past decades shifted from a social democratic system to market individualism. The shift has put pressure on universities to justify their increased expenditures. In this situation, humanities scholars have simply not been good enough at explaining the value of the work they do. Much like St. Augustine's celebrated confession that he felt he knew what time was, but was at a loss to explain it when put on the spot, humanities scholars have long taken the value of the humanities for granted. When asked to name it, however, we have stumbled and stuttered or taken refuge in noble abstractions. The present situation is a good opportunity to reflect more systematically about the humanities and their socio-political position, not only in order to provide better descriptions to appease deans, politicians, funders, and voters, but also to realize, to map, and to make visible the many ways and channels through which humanist scholarship shapes the world around us.

Beyond interpretation

If a socio-political perspective on the humanities points to the necessity of speaking differently and more effectively about the role of the humanities in the world, what insights might a philosophical perspective bring to the topic? As mentioned above, the idea that the humanities are fundamentally different from other forms of scientific inquiry has a long pedigree. Dilthey's distinction between different modes of inquiry in the natural sciences and in the humanities has since developed into a sharp division. The establishment of the conceptual entity of 'the humanities' in the 1940s and 1950s, the often quite ugly 'Two Cultures' debate about the relationship between the two disciplines initiated by C.P. Snow and F.R. Leavis in the 1960s, and the present opposition between STEM fields and the humanities have only deepened the perceived divide within the scientific world.

But does this division accurately account for the type of work that is actually conducted in the humanities and in the natural sciences? What do humanist scholars *do*? What are their research methods? And are their methods and aims fundamentally different from those of the natural sciences? As Onora O'Neill shows in her essay 'The Humanities Beyond Interpretation', humanist scholars also seek explanations for vast arrays of empirical material, just as interpretation is a fundamental mode of inquiry in the natural sciences. Conversely, parts of mathematics and theoretical physics are closer to the ideal of a pure science disconnected from any worldly demands in the form of impact or concrete applications than much work performed in linguistics, history, or literary studies. The consolidation of the social sciences in the twentieth century has been described as the emergence of a 'third culture' wedged between the humanities and the sciences,[7] but it might be more accurate to say that instead of two or three there are more than two hundred cultures or, simply, one culture.[8]

As O'Neill makes clear, once we subject the alleged division of the sciences to closer scrutiny, we are forced to abandon any sharp dichotomies when it comes to both scientific method and societal impact. Not only are interpretation and explanation present in both areas and often deployed simultaneously; scientific praxis cannot be reduced to these two modes of inquiry. Scholars often make claims that are neither explanatory nor interpretive. They make claims not about what the world *is*, but about what the world *ought to be*. Such normative judgements do not seek to describe the world, but to realize certain standards and thereby to change the world in some way or other. If we simply adhere to entrenched ideas about distinct domains with their distinct methods, we will miss the methodological pluralism that informs research across the whole scientific field. While the emphases may vary, the humanities, at this level, is not a foreign country where things are done differently. Its scientific customs are recognizable throughout the world of science.

Changing the world

We may encounter little opposition to the idea that the modes of humanistic inquiry belong wholly within the world of science. But while the natural sciences result in patents, new technologies, and visible changes to our societies and the way we live, the results of humanistic inquiry remain enclosed within a small circle of savants without leaving much of an imprint on the wider world and its inhabitants. We might easily imagine a world without the humanities, a world that would tick along without any noticeable difference. A deep historical perspective quickly dispels such fantasies.

In a grand overview, Rens Bod's essay 'How the Humanities Have Changed the World' points to numerous examples of the very direct impact of humanities scholarship both on the other sciences and outside of the scientific realm. As the case of Panini and John Backus shows, it was the findings of a humanities field – linguistics – that enabled the development of information technology. But the examples are legion. In the 1950s, the life sciences also turned to linguistics when they came to regard the genome as a textual information system; so did twentieth-century molecular biology. Nineteenth-century stemmatic philology inspired the latter, which adopted both the structure of the tree of texts (stemma) and several of the rules that philologists employed to work on them. In other words, humanistic discoveries and inventions were transposed from their field of origin into adjacent fields where they served as direct templates for understanding information theory, computer science, cybernetics, and genetics. If we turn to art history, the description of linear perspective by Leon Battista Alberti in 1435 fundamentally changed how we see the world and led to a transformation of architecture. And as for history proper, source criticism, which can be traced all the way back to Herodotus and Thucydides, forms a central tool at the International Court of Justice to distinguish between authentic sources and forgeries. Not only is the history of science incomplete and incomprehensible without a proper assessment of the humanistic inventions that have been taken up and variously applied or developed by the other sciences; fundamental activities and institutions in our society would not be able to function without them.

As Bod's numerous examples make clear, the humanities have produced a vast reservoir of knowledge of remarkable durability. Developments, discoveries, and inventions made hundreds or even thousands of years ago are picked up, recontextualized, and retooled by the natural and technical sciences that then get the credit for the patents, contraptions, and insights that change the way we live. But much of it emerges from the reservoir of knowledge that humanist scholars have produced over the years and that flows into other scientific fields and societal institutions through multiple channels, following often circuitous routes. Evidently, not all breakthroughs in the humanities have a direct and measurable, if belated, impact. But by tracing such routes, Bod offers a complementary perspective on humanistic knowledge production. Linguistics, art history, literary studies, history, and musicology not only describe and interpret the expressions of human thoughts and actions – they also solve concrete problems and make actual progress.[9] And even if some scholarship may at times appear esoteric, say the study of the backsides of jewels from Egyptian pharaonic graves, that scholar is most likely also engaged in teaching, whereby the exemplarity – methodologically, theoretically, and conceptually – of this material is passed on to students. Through exposure to many both obscure and recognizable studies, students may then carry such research into their future careers in private companies, municipalities, media, or politics.

By bringing these three essays together, this book seeks to accomplish two aims. First, it serves as a succinct guide for students, scholars, administrators, and the wider reading public who seek an introduction to the humanities and to their status in contemporary society. Second, it articulates a more world-oriented narrative of what the humanities are and what they do.

By asking us to rethink how we *talk about* the humanities, what *doing* humanistic research entails, and what the concrete *impact* of the humanities is, the ideas in this book challenge conventional notions of the alleged isolationism and practical insignificance of humanities research. Instead, they point to the myriad ways in which the humanities are situated in the world and have both engaged and changed it. Spotlighting these often invisible connections, and articulating better the practical dealings across the wide territory between the myth of the ivory tower and the myth of salvation, the book will at least present us with a more accurate picture of what goes on in the humanities today.

We would like to thank the Carlsberg Foundation for its generous support of this book.

References

1 See Rens Bod's essay in this volume. See also *A New History of the Humanities: The Search for Principles and Patterns from Antiquity to the Present* (Oxford: Oxford University Press, 2013); and *Een Wereld Vol Patronen: De Geschiedenis van Kennis* (Amsterdam: Prometheus, 2019).
2 https://www.insidehighered.com/news/2017/06/05/analysis-finds-significant-drop-humanities-majors-gains-liberal-arts-degrees (retrieved 24 October 2019).
3 http://mapping-humanities.dk/_pdf/rapporter/Humanomics-2018-Humanistiske-universitetsforskeres-vidensformidling-og-videnssamarbejde.pdf (retrieved 24 October 2019).
4 Collini, *What are Universities for?* (London: Penguin, 2012), p.63. See also Helen Small, *The Value of the Humanities* (Oxford: Oxford University Press, 2013), p.14.
5 See e.g. Wilhelm Dilthey, *Einleitung in die Geisteswissenschaften: Versuch einer Grundlegung für das Studium der Gesellschaft und der Geschichte* (Leipzig: Duncker & Humblot, 1883).
6 Small, *The Value of the Humanities*, p.152.
7 Wolf Lepenies, *Between Literature and Science: The Rise of Sociology* (Cambridge: Cambridge University Press, 1992).
8 Stefan Collini, Introductory essay to C.P. Snow, *The Two Cultures* (Cambridge: Cambridge University Press, 1993), p.xliv.
9 See also Rens Bod, *A New History of the Humanities*.

On Not "Justifying" the Humanities

Stefan Collini
University of Cambridge

I

Attempts to extend and deepen our understanding of the human past, or to probe and analyze the profoundest puzzles of existence, or to sharpen and enrich our appreciation of literary and other artistic creations – these are self-evidently interesting and worthwhile activities. Nothing is gained by pretending that we think these are in some way unintelligible or alien or worthless activities. We can, if we wish, affect to take the role of the village reductionist and pretend to believe that the only indisputably legitimate activities are those that put food in the stomach or a shelter over the head or money in the bank, but it is not a pose we can sustain for long. It soon becomes evident that we have minds and thoughts and reflections and curiosity, and therefore that we are drawn into the kinds of activities I identified in my opening sentence.

Of course, no-one does all these things all the time, nor does each of us do our chosen activities with the same degree of intensity or perseverance or ability, but there is nothing remotely puzzling in the idea that some people will wish to attend to some of these things some of the time. And in support of that truth we might mention that there is a very long, rich, and well-documented history of human beings doing just that. What can it mean, therefore, to be asked to 'justify' these activities? What are the values or lemmas that could count as providing a justification for these fundamental human enterprises? And, focusing on the theme of this volume, do they need to be justified to *you* or to *me*?

I begin like this because we all know that discussions about 'the humanities' in contemporary society are, implicitly or explicitly, driven by the felt need to find 'justifications' for doing them.[1] It would be silly to deny that there are social, cultural, and financial pressures that encourage this quest. I take those pressures seriously and I believe that as academics in these disciplines we cannot simply ignore them. But that, I think, makes it all the more important to identify clearly what the terms of the questions are and what could count as persuasive answers for particular audiences.

Almost any event or discussion with 'the humanities' in its title risks seeming both predictable and depressing. Predictable because we suspect that, after running through various travails and accusations, the humanities will by the end emerge in their full redemptive glory as the indispensable means of living a satisfactory human life (and as the grand and pious adjectives pile up it becomes hard to suppress a yawn). And depressing because, despite the inevitable arrival of the 'deepest human values' cavalry to save the day at the end, the story along the way is always one of being beleaguered and besieged, involving a tone that varies somewhere between the self-justifying and the complaining.

Since I do not wish to encourage this tone, I shall take a rather quizzical look at both the activity of 'justifying' and the category of 'the humanities' in an attempt to scrub away some of the congealed abstractions. I shall then quickly suggest one or two ways of engaging in this public discourse that are less defensive and more specific. Obviously, the greater part of my own direct experience relates to the situation in Britain, and I am certainly not presuming that this applies in any simple way to the very different public cultures and the much more diverse higher education systems in the rest of the world. But there are some trends and elements here which, if not strictly speaking global, are already common to Britain and the USA and other parts of the world, and which may soon be coming to many countries of continental Europe.

We should surely begin by acknowledging that at present, books and essays 'justifying' the value of the humanities are largely read by those who believe in the case already. There can be, I believe, a value in animating and fortifying beliefs that we may otherwise take for granted or lose confidence in, but it should be clear that scholars in the humanities are not principally being asked to 'justify' *to each other* the interesting-ness or worthwhileness of the study and teaching of the humanities disciplines. Rather, we are being asked to make a case in response to a set of more limited and practical questions, perhaps about courses of study, numbers of students, types of research, and, above all, the expenditure of public money. But once we recognize *that*, we can see, first, that the cases we make will have to be entirely context-dependent and at a much lower level of abstraction; and second, that 'the humanities' may not be the most useful category to employ here.

Let me start with a very obvious point about how justification is, in practice, highly context-dependent. It depends, first, on the kind of criticism or scepticism which is being responded to or at least anticipated; and, second, it always depends upon being able to establish some commonality of values somewhere, some bridgehead in even the most hostile critic's assumptions, if the attempt at justification is to gain any purchase at all. For these reasons, it does not seem to me very helpful to try to develop some all-purpose justification couched in highly abstract terms: it may be better to think of particular forms of resistance we want to overcome on the part of particular publics (often in comparison to particular other preferred activities or purposes), and this means that the form and argumentative strategy of our exercises in characterization and persuasion need to be tailored accordingly. The relevant publics may, as we know, include various categories – legislators, students, parents, foundation administrators, journalists, schoolchildren, colleagues, donors, government officials, taxpayers, and so on – and of course any actual individual may belong to more than one of these categories.

Quite a lot of the well-meaning statements that are issued about the humanities tend to reduce to a series of abstract nouns, in which 'imagination', 'empathy', and the other usual suspects invariably figure. Justification at this level of abstraction may have its uses, but one obvious weakness of this strategy is that it is fatally easy for any interlocutors to enthusiastically concur with these large-sounding claims while not actually being persuaded about, or conceding anything to, the more local or institutional or financial case that the claims are meant to support. Government ministers, for example, can all too easily endorse grand statements about the value of the humanities in affirming our sense of the human while simultaneously imposing large budget cuts on humanities funding.

Another, perhaps slightly less obvious weakness, is that such high-flown claims do not seem to entail the array of often knotty, detailed, and usually empirical enquiries that make up the actual daily practices of scholars in our various disciplines. The most elevated claims for the humanities end up sounding as though their goals could be met if everyone would just spend their time reading *The Odyssey* and *King Lear* with an open heart. Not only is that kind of thing too general to be useful in most actual situations where persuasion is needed, but also it fails to focus on what most scholars in humanities disciplines actually do most of the time.

Turning to the category of 'the humanities' itself, the first thing to say is that obviously it is chiefly an organizational or classifying term, and that is, of course, one reason why it may be a mistake to be too essentialist about it. We should certainly not speak as though it were a timeless category. Not only is it a term that did not come into general currency in its modern sense in English until the mid-twentieth century, but it did so largely by way of reaction to the imperial claims of the methodological positivism of the 1930s and 1940s as supposedly embodied in the natural and the social sciences.

Perhaps it has never quite shaken off the aura of conservatism and defensiveness that were inherited from these origins, and it seems to me important not to endorse either of those associations. I should just add that although the term has been well established in Britain for some decades, it is fair to say that the discourse about 'the humanities' has had, and continues to have, a particularly intimate connection with the characteristically American conception of a 'liberal arts' education largely made up of elective courses. Indeed, some scholars have recently made the case that the very category of 'the humanities' is intimately bound up with a particular educational version of 'the American dream'.[2]

Secondly, even in the present the increased use of this English-language label risks importing a false universality. Not only is the term not native to various other cultural traditions – it is not, after all, identical to the *'sciences humaines'* or the *'Geisteswissenschaften'* – but its over-confident use also conceals wide variations in institutional arrangements even within a single cultural tradition. Sometimes History is placed among the social sciences, sometimes not; sometimes Art and Music are placed in art schools and conservatoires, or sometimes separately classified as 'creative or performing arts', separate from the humanities; sometimes Religious Studies are included, sometimes those are the preserve of Divinity Schools and seminaries; sometimes Linguistics, or the more cultural aspects of Sociology and Anthropology are included, sometimes they are firmly identified as social sciences; even Philosophy's membership of the club is sometimes questioned, especially those aspects of it which are closer to logic or mathematics and far removed from the records of human activity; and so on. These classifications vary even across the English-speaking world, and still more across cultures with different intellectual and educational traditions.

A third reason to be careful about too readily using the category of 'the humanities' is the risk that we may inadvertently re-instate some version of the supposed 'two cultures' divide.[3] For many intellectual and practical purposes, it is a mistake to speak as though there were some clear-cut and exhaustive divide between 'the humanities' and 'the natural sciences'. Great swathes of work in all disciplines are broadly analytical and factual in similar ways, where standards of accuracy, rigour, and evidence are closely related. What all the disciplines share is at least as important as what differentiates them, and they all have much to gain by articulating their common interest in the university as an enterprise devoted principally to the extension and deepening of human understanding.

And fourth, another way in which treating 'the humanities' as a single intellectual enterprise risks misleading us is that it almost always ends up focusing on 'the great books', and usually, therefore, reducing our diverse disciplines to the study of a few classics of literature and philosophy. But even in literature and philosophy, and still more in other fields, most scholars most of the time are not reading the great books but are engaging in some much more analytical or empirical enquiries concentrated on particular times and places, and our account of humanities disciplines should reflect this. The scholar who is attempting to decipher the fragmentary shards left by a now-extinct civilization, or the scholar who is using parish registers to work out typical household structures in seventeenth-century England, or the scholar who is charting the representation of gender roles in recent

Latin-American films – these are more representative of actual practice in our disciplines and our descriptions should be tailored to reflect this.

Constantly emphasizing the category of 'the humanities' does not just operate at too high a level of abstraction: by flattening out the distinctiveness of individual disciplines it tends to lose what may be most impressive and persuasive about a good piece of work in, say, Ancient History or Renaissance Musicology or criticism of the nineteenth-century Russian novel, and so on. Individual disciplines, after all, are not merely accidents of institutional arrangements: there are long and rich cultural traditions behind thinking about literature or religion or art and so on, and it should be possible to harness the strength of those traditions to support the standing of the current forms of these enquiries. So, as a matter of tactics, it can often be more productive to try to illustrate what is valuable about work in, say, metaphysics in *its* terms, and in literary criticism in *its* terms, and in social history in *its* terms, and so on.

This should also help us not to be led into making exaggerated claims for the moral benefits of studying these disciplines: some defenders of the humanities are, in my view, a little too prone to speak as though their study is bound to make us all into morally superior beings, a claim which is surely vulnerable to some rather disturbing counter-evidence (as a glance down the average departmental corridor will readily suggest). So, instead of digging ourselves in behind a stockade of over-ambitious claims couched at too high a level of abstraction and delivered in a tone of defensiveness, it is usually better, when identifying the character and role of these enterprises, to start from some of the facts of our actual practice in our particular, diverse disciplines and work up from there.

All these are reasons for caution, even perhaps for scepticism. But let me also make two more positive points in this connection. First, as scholars, we do need to make a greater effort to try to provide politicians, officials, journalists, administrators, and other public figures with a usable set of *descriptions* of what we do – note, I say 'descriptions', not 'justifications'. However, we should not get sucked in to the trap of claiming that the main value of these activities lies in the indirect contribution they may make to economic growth. It is tempting to put all our eggs in this basket when we are dealing directly with governments because economic growth is the one goal which is assumed to have indisputable electoral legitimacy in market democracies. But there are two risks here.

First, there is the risk that, in time, only those activities that can be shown to contribute in this way will come to be supported, excluding those that are harder to justify in these terms. And second, there is the risk that we ourselves come to inhabit this language, that we start to understand the value of what we do in these terms and even start to choose research projects or teaching approaches accordingly. If you think I am exaggerating this risk, you should look at the effect of the 'impact' requirement in the UK's research assessment exercise as an example of what happens if we allow an external vocabulary of *justification* to come to provide an internal criterion of *quality*. In that exercise, departments must demonstrate the non-academic 'impact' of their research, and this then becomes a major determinant of the ranking assigned to the *quality* of that research, with the result that some scholars are now starting to choose to work on the kinds of topic that might generate evidence of the right kind of social and economic impact.

My second point is that alarmism, defensiveness, and the alienation of public support are closely related. There are, as I have said, many publics, and we should not underestimate the level of interest in and enthusiasm for work in humanities disciplines in various quarters of society. Among several of these publics there is an instinctive recognition that unfettered intellectual enquiry is central to what universities are about, and therefore there is, potentially, a much greater reservoir of interest in, and latent appreciation of, the work of universities than the narrow and instrumental official discourse about 'economic growth' ever succeeds in tapping into.

Moreover, the evidence from sources as diverse as literary festivals, TV documentaries, book sales, gallery visits, and so on suggests that many people are already interested in questions about literature and history, philosophy and religion, art and music, so it should not be impossible, while steering well clear of the misguided notion of 'impact', to persuade them of the value of developing more systematic understanding in these areas. The best work in the humanities disciplines does this brilliantly and we should not sell such work short by misrepresenting it as an indirect way of developing commercially useful skills. If we do, we are getting ourselves into the absurd position of justifying learning to play Beethoven's piano sonatas on the grounds that it helps to make us better typists.

II

At this point, it may help to consider the question of justification historically, and this may be best done by looking at the claims that have been made for a particular discipline. I shall take the study of literature as my example, partly because it is my own area of expertise but partly also because it seems to be the discipline that is most given to bouts of agonized self-examination as it casts about for usable justifications of its activities. As far as I know, these rather ritualized moves do not play such a large part in the proceedings of most other disciplines. There do not seem to be endless meditations on, say, 'Astrophysics and the making of the democratic citizen', or jeremiads with titles like 'Whither inorganic chemistry?' Almost all disciplines will from time to time have panics about falling student numbers, gripes about diminished funding, and calls for paradigm shifts and theoretical renewals. But the repeated public scrutinies of their discipline undertaken by scholars of English literature do seem peculiarly expressive of a recognizable blend of anxiety and defensiveness backed up by high-toned self-justifications.

Having worked for some time on the history of English as an academic subject, I would say that there have been six main impulses or arguments used to promote its establishment and growth:

1. The impulse to make literature an object of exact knowledge on a similar footing to other topics.
2. The impulse to construct an inspiring genealogy, whether in national, ethnic, gender, or other terms.
3. The impulse to nurture the imagination by cultivating an informed familiarity with the range and power of literature.
4. The impulse to train critical readers, both to read other kinds of writing and to 'read' other forms of cultural expression.
5. The impulse to provide a version of moral education, developing empathy and making us better people.
6. The impulse to develop skills that will be useful across later forms of employment.

It is not quite true that these six impulses appeared in exactly this order from the mid-nineteenth century to the present, but there is something of a chronological sequence here. Partly the sequence reflects intellectual fashions, but very largely it reflects pressures from outside the discipline for justifications of what may seem the otherwise indefensibly enjoyable and useless activity of reading literature in the vernacular. Clearly, there is a tendency for the justifications to oscillate between what we might demotically call the 'deathbed test' and the 'paying the rent' test. Less obviously, there is a curious tension between what literary scholars actually spend most of their time doing and what they *say* they do when they are, as it were, put in the witness box. Everyday practice is largely about exact knowledge and better understanding of particular pieces of literature. Set-piece justifications are largely about social utility and the expansion of our humanity. This is a revealing asymmetry, one that underlines the need to attend to the heterogeneity of actual scholarly practices rather than to couch a would-be 'justification' in the most abstract terms.

When academics are holding forth on the 'value' of the study of English now we tend to hear more about how, say, *Hard Times* expands our sympathies, or *Macbeth* teaches us about the pitfalls of ambition, than about the manuscript circulation of Elizabethan sonnets or references to new technology in Edwardian novels, even though the latter two examples are much more representative of what English scholars actually do with their working days than the first two. Much of the 'work' that scholars in English do is, methodologically or even epistemologically, continuous with that done in most other disciplines in the university; this is one reason why it seems to me that, if we do feel driven to engage in characterizations of the nature of certain kinds of intellectual labour, then the enterprise to be argued for is the university itself.

'English' is, of course, simply one local expression of the larger category of 'literature', and many of the arguments mentioned above can be found in the histories of cognate literary subjects as well. When, towards the end of the First World War, the British government commissioned enquiries on the place of Classics, English, and Modern Languages in the national education system, the resulting reports had, not surprisingly, a good deal of common ground. The cases that were made for all three disciplines depended heavily on a shared understanding of the ideal of 'culture' and the prestige of 'literature' as a humanizing force.[4] This was to be understood, according to the companion report on Modern Languages, as the development of "the higher faculties, the imagination, the sense of beauty and the intellectual comprehension, clear vision, mental harmony, a just sense of proportion, higher illumination".[5] Such justifications rarely exhibit an excess of modesty.

One of the major cultural shifts which Classics and

English as well as Modern Languages have had to reckon with in the late twentieth and early twenty-first centuries is the decline in the standing and centrality of literature. In the Victorian period, the most elevated case for the Classics was made in moral and aesthetic terms: Victorian Hellenism, in particular, stressed the civilizing effect of an intimate acquaintance with Ancient Greek ideals of the True, the Good, and the Beautiful. In roughly the first two thirds of the twentieth century, the main argument had to shift to the justification of Latin, as the increasingly dominant component of Classics, and that emphasized its unmatchable value as a form of mental training. From the 1970s and 1980s onwards, the case has tended to be put more in terms of an acquaintance with 'the Classical tradition' and with ancient societies as peculiarly educative forms of sociological and historical diversity. Justifications tend to exhibit a striking plasticity, in response both to changes in the disciplines themselves and, even more, to wider societal expectations.

Justifications for the study and teaching of literature in the vernacular have exhibited a comparable adaptiveness, though here there is a form or aspect of work that has long been considered central but that is now being more and more squeezed out by the managerial imperatives of the contemporary university. If the term were not open to so much misunderstanding, I would be inclined to call it 'critical judgement', not meaning thereby the unremitting focus of identifying aesthetic value and ranking works that allegedly contain that mysterious quality, but the more everyday activity of arriving at a characterization and assessment of a piece of writing which is not entirely determined by the accumulation of factual knowledge about it.

Increasingly, we are driven by current categories to classify what we do when we are not teaching or administering as 'research'. But this category brings with it assumptions that fit some subjects better than others, and the two it fits least well, though perhaps for slightly different reasons, are Philosophy and English, where some of the activities constitutive of those two disciplines do not necessarily issue 'outputs' that contain 'new findings' (or, as we put it in our contaminated dialect in the UK, items that are 'REFfable'). We could say that part of what gets left out is 'scholarship'; we could, if we want to be gently mocked, simply call it 'wide reading'; we could even, if we want to be sneered at as elitist and undemocratic, call it 'cultivation'. But, however we describe it, the absence of this fundamental activity will mean that we tend to do the two officially recognized activities – teaching and research – rather badly. Somebody who writes, let us say, a readable, critically alert, well-informed introduction to a significant literary work in a series such as Oxford World's Classics may exhibit the strengths of the discipline far better than the excavation of some strained and minor historical connection of the kind that assessment and promotion procedures count as 'an original contribution to knowledge'. But all the institutional pressures – not just regimes of research assessment but also appointments, promotions, and the demands of professionalism – tell against such work and against the exercise of accumulated critical judgement that it represents.

Let me make clear that specialization is essential and not to be apologized for: it is the hallmark of every serious collective intellectual enquiry and there is no reason to expect a wider public to read most of our specialized publications. I have no sympathy at all with the ritualistic MLA-bashing on grounds of the abstruse titles of many of the papers. Let me also emphasize that I am not recommending the misshapen monster that is 'impact' in its current REF form. But I am suggesting that, alongside other 'work' that scholars of English literature do, cultivating an alert and widely informed responsiveness to the quiddities of different pieces of writing has a continuing place in our activities, even if others might jib at my brief description of it. In the study of literature, the extension and deepening of understanding involves more than just the conjunction of theory plus historical knowledge, but we often have difficulty in identifying and speaking up for what this further element is.

One additional benefit of giving adequate recognition to such broadly critical writing is that it helps to keep our lines of communication open with varieties of non-specialist, non-student readers interested in and curious about literature. If we allow our 'work' to be defined exclusively in terms of 'teaching' and 'research', we may obtain short-term managerial approval, but we risk forfeiting the interest of that much larger constituency whose support may, in the long run, be more important. So, more generally, I am suggesting that the 'scientific' model of research and publication tends to narrow or misdescribe what we do in one direction, while the simultaneously defensive yet over-ambitious justifications for 'the humanities' tend to misrepresent what we do in the opposite direction.

III

Everything I have discussed so far deals with questions of argument, presentation, and persuasion. I want now to turn to a different level of analysis, but one which I believe supports my sceptical conclusions about the value of justifications for the humanities that are couched in overly general terms. I want to look at some facts concerning the position of humanities disciplines in universities in Europe and the United States over the past two or three generations. We may begin with the question of student enrolments, that is, the choices that applicants and then undergraduate students make about which courses of study to follow. A lot of good work has recently been done on this by historians such as Roger Geiger in the USA and Peter Mandler in Britain.[6] Their research shows that, despite repeated alarms about an alleged 'crisis of the humanities', student numbers in the humanities did not in fact show any catastrophic decline in the years between 1945 and 2010; if anything, the reverse was the case, though there were many local variations.

Several factors contributed to this. One was the increasing feminization of the student body over these years, with female students somewhat more likely than males to choose humanities subjects, especially languages, literature, and art. Another enormously important factor was the perception that employers believed a good education in humanities subjects was a suitable preparation for the forms of employment in which they were trying to recruit. This was not a straightforward matter, and in some cases the perception may not have corresponded to the reality, but as long as students believed that they would not be penalized in the job market for having studied humanities subjects, then the enrolment numbers held up.

And a third big determinant was what happened in schools. Some of the major disciplines such as history and literature have been central to secondary school education across these decades, which encouraged numbers of students to study these subjects at university. We can see how decisive this factor can be by looking at the decision of the British government in the early 2000s to make the study of a modern foreign language no longer compulsory in secondary education. This had a dramatic impact on numbers choosing to do degrees in modern languages, to the extent that the university-level study of literature in all European languages other than French and Spanish is now almost at risk of dying out, though there are also longer-term cultural causes for their shrinkage.

There are some broad patterns common to most European and European-influenced societies where the expansion of higher education is concerned in the second half of the twentieth century and the first decade of the twenty-first. One common feature is that new institutions that were founded in these years with the intention of developing a new educational model increasingly came to imitate the dominant established models, though usually without the same status. Up until at least the 1980s or 1990s this pattern favoured humanities disciplines because they were seen to be one of the defining characteristics of the traditional institutions. Another common feature is that the first phases of this expansion, especially in the 1960s and 1970s, largely increased the recruitment from the same advantaged sections of society. The most significant change in these years was the big increase in the numbers of daughters as well as sons of the middle class who went into higher education, another development which, as I mentioned, favoured the humanities disciplines, or at least some of them. Recruitment on a large scale from the less privileged social strata only really started to happen in the 1990s and 2000s.

If the pattern of student enrolment was broadly

positive for the humanities up to 2000 or even 2010, it may be that we have been starting to see a change over the past six or seven years (and especially the last two years), though it is too early to say how marked or how permanent the apparent decline in numbers of humanities students may be. But here, too, scholarly research offers some useful longer perspectives. There is, for example, some evidence to suggest that the higher the proportion of the age cohort that is enrolled in higher education in any given country, the lower the proportion studying humanities subjects will be. Moreover, the figures suggest that the higher concentrations of humanities students will be found in the most selective institutions, even if lower-status institutions offer the same range of subjects.[7]

Many elements come into play here, including that students from more privileged backgrounds are more likely to see a degree in a humanities subject as the consolidation of advantages in terms of cultural capital, whereas those from social strata new to higher education are more likely to be anxious that they will need relevant expert qualifications for the job market if they are to compensate for having attended less highly regarded universities. (Interestingly, in the UK, the evidence suggests that the top employers are more influenced by the perceived standing of the university that job applicants attended than by the subject they studied, a tendency that may work to the benefit of humanities subjects in so-called 'elite' institutions while also helping to reproduce social advantage.) Indeed, a more specific worry that we might have in this connection at present is that students, and eventually scholars, in many of these disciplines are increasingly likely to be recruited from the offspring of the privileged classes. This is already true to a considerable extent of disciplines such as Art History and Classics in Britain, and is becoming true of Modern Languages.

Overall, however, the point to emphasize here is that the evidence does not suggest that student enrolment is noticeably responsive to large-scale statements about the value of the humanities, but, rather, that it is determined by a range of more substantial social and economic factors. In 1964 a once-celebrated book was published entitled *Crisis in the Humanities*, in which the distinguished contributors announced that these disciplines were on the brink of extinction unless they radically mended their ways.[8] In practice, this announcement of a near-terminal crisis was made just as one of the largest expansions of numbers of both scholars and students in the humanities that there has ever been was getting under way. Clearly, we should not exaggerate the causal role of such pronouncements, either in the past or in the present.

Taking a wider perspective still, we shall of course hear more in the immediate future about the need for a global view, though it is important to recognize that the relation of many humanities disciplines to their native cultures will always remain more intimate than that of other disciplines. Most work in the natural sciences, and even in many of the social sciences, can be pursued anywhere and in a global economy will, by and large, be pursued where funding dictates, but the study and teaching of, say, Danish history is always likely to be particularly pursued in Denmark, or Portuguese literature in Portugal, and so on. And this is a reminder from another angle that these enquiries are more continuous with interests and debates in the wider non-academic culture of which they are a part. The future of, for example, art history will be considerably affected by what happens to galleries and collections, the future of the study of literature by what happens to literary publishing and literary journalism, and so on. A narrow focus on funding policies for undergraduate education risks losing sight of some of the forces that give these subjects their vitality and wider appeal in particular cultures.

IV

Looking to the future, my guess is that in terms of numbers (of both students and staff) and in terms of their influence on decisions about processes and structures in universities, the humanities disciplines are likely to be a more reduced presence, absolutely as well as relatively, in higher education systems in 2050 and beyond, where they may largely be confined to the major research universities and the more elite colleges. Certainly, they will not recover the centrality they had in the middle decades of the twentieth century. In Britain, but not in Britain alone, business and management studies is by now the single most popular subject at undergraduate level, a development that clearly reflects wider changes in society over the past two or three decades, and there is every reason to think those changes will continue. It is also the case that the democratization of higher education in most countries has seen the traditional academic subjects, whether in the humanities or the natural sciences, being less popular among the social groups now entering higher education for the first time, and the decline in the position of such disciplines in the newer institutions that primarily cater to these groups is particularly marked (though, interestingly, the subject choices of black and minority ethnic women may be a partial exception to this generalization).

But nothing is forever. A hundred and fifty years ago many would have found it unthinkable that Classics could ever lose its dominant place in education, and some would have regarded such a prospect as the end of civilization. Something similar is now being said about other humanities subjects. I do not think we should encourage such apocalyptic or alarmist talk. Outstanding scholarship in these disciplines will continue to be published (whatever 'published' comes to mean), and there will still be substantial demand for courses in them. We should not regard the mere fact that a smaller *proportion* of students may take courses in the humanities as spelling disaster. The shifting proportions are, after all, reflective of deeper changes in the character of our societies and the humanities should certainly not be positioned as attempting to resist all such changes.

The *contemporary political expression* of some of these changes is another matter. At present, we may be witnessing a shift from the university as shaped by the social democratic era to the university as reflecting the era of the politics of market individualism. From the mid-nineteenth through to the late twentieth century, one of the notable achievements of European and European-influenced societies was the way they managed to adapt the attenuated traditions of their then few and rather marginal institutions of higher learning to turn them into powerhouses of national culture, and the humanities disciplines prospered accordingly. Both aristocratic and social democratic values in turn contributed to this transformation. But from at least the 1980s onwards, other values have been more dominant and are in the process of re-shaping universities in their own image. In these circumstances it would be unrealistic to expect the humanities disciplines to be able to continue to benefit from the older kind of deference to the ideals of 'culture'. Debates on the theme of the place (or nature or value or future) of 'the humanities' are one name we give to our anxieties about this transition.

Still, we should not let these political pressures drive us into misdescribing the purpose of learning more about history or literature or philosophy. This is one of the places where the logic of justification can lead us astray. There is a tendency for defenders of universities in general and the humanities in particular to want to present them as contributing to every approved social good. This tendency seems to me a mistake both as a matter of fact and as a matter of tactics. We may believe that 'social mobility', whatever we think that means, is a good thing, and we may believe that 'respecting the views of less privileged groups', whatever we think that means, is also a good thing, but we would be foolish to try to justify the study of the humanities in terms of these larger social goals, which can at best be by-products of the work of a university, not its defining aim. We may certainly hope that in helping to extend cultural understanding we are not narrowing human sympathies, but there may be no *necessary* connection in either direction. The fact that someone can make a dazzling breakthrough in the understanding of human behaviour while at the same time behaving abominably in other aspects of life and holding deplorable political views may make us uncomfortable, but it is a combination that universities have to live with because such extension of understanding is their primary activity, not the manufacturing of right-mindedness.

To avoid misunderstanding, let me repeat that I believe it is very important that historians try to demonstrate to wider audiences something of the appeal and interest of the best work in history, and that scholars of literature do this for literary studies and philosophers do it for philosophy and so on. I would urge that as scholars and teachers we need to do more of this, not less. But well-meant official statements by those representing universities that attempt to 'justify' these disciplines on the grounds that they are an excellent preparation for becoming a corporate executive or hedge-fund manager or on the grounds that, through the 'culture industries', they help to boost GDP, risk undermining rather than strengthening our position. Rather than falling into this trap, it may be better to acknowledge that there are limits to how successfully we can persuade certain sections of the political and media worlds about the value of what we do.

The truth is that the humanities form a relatively small part of the modern research university, but they bulk very large in all discussions about the 'idea' or 'future' of universities. This may not simply be because those who dilate on these matters are drawn disproportionately from humanities disciplines. It may in part be because the discourse about the humanities has become a locus – and in some respects a placeholder – for wider anxieties about the changing relations between culture and democracy, between society and economy. These anxieties have real objects as well as, like all anxieties, their exaggerated or phantasmatic features, but in this brief discussion I have tried not to encourage this only partly conscious use of the category of 'the humanities' as a way of addressing these wider issues, not least because it tends to make so much of the discourse about the humanities simultaneously too defensive and too pious. We have good reason, in my view, to be more modest, but then, I believe, we have every reason also to be more confident.

*Some paragraphs of this essay first appeared, in an earlier form, in my *Speaking of Universities* (London: Verso, 2017).

References

1 There is a vast literature here. Perhaps one of the best known recent statements is Martha C. Nussbaum, *Not For Profit: Why Democracy Needs the Humanities* (Princeton: Princeton University Press, 2010); for an attempt to make the case in more practical terms, see Donald Drakeman, *Why We Need the Humanities: Life Science, Law and the Common Good* (Basingstoke: Palgrave, 2016). The most careful and penetrating analysis of the historical and philosophical roots of such arguments is Helen Small, *The Value of the Humanities* (Oxford: Oxford University Press, 2013).
2 Geoffrey Harpham, *The Humanities and the Dream of America* (Chicago: University of Chicago Press, 2011). See also Louis Menand, 'The humanities revolution', in his *The Marketplace of Ideas: Reform and Resistance in the American University* (New York: Norton, 2010).
3 For reservations about this concept, see my introduction in C.P. Snow, *The Two Cultures*, ed. Stefan Collini (Cambridge: Cambridge University Press, 1993).
4 *The Teaching of English in England* (London: HMSO, 1921), popularly known as 'The Newbolt Report' after its chairman, Sir Henry Newbolt, drew particularly heavily on this line of argument, but it also emphasized a nationalist pride in her-

itage, as well as more pragmatic considerations such as the accessibility of English to large numbers not exposed to the study of Classics and its role in teaching students to write well.

5 *Modern Studies: Being the Report of the Committee on the Position of Modern Languages in the Educational System of Great Britain* (London: HMSO, 1918), p.47. See Susan Bayley, 'Modern languages: an "ideal of humane learning": the Leathes Report of 1918', *Journal of Educational Administration and History*, 23 (1991), pp.11-24. This report was similarly known by the name of its chairman, Sir Stanley Leathes.

6 See Roger L. Geiger, 'Demography and curriculum: the humanities in American higher education from the 1950s through the 1980s', in David A. Hollinger (ed.), *The Humanities and the Dynamics of Inclusion since World War II* (Baltimore: Johns Hopkins University Press, 2006); Geiger, 'Postmortem for the current era: change in American higher education, 1980-2010', Penn State University, Center for the Study of Higher Education, CSHE working paper 3, July 2010. Peter Mandler, 'Educating the nation: II, universities', and 'Educating the nation: IV, subject choice', *Transactions of the Royal Historical Society*, 6th ser., XXV (2015), pp.1-26, and XXVII (2017), pp.1-27.

7 For these points, see Geiger, 'Demography and curriculum', esp. pp.64-69.

8 J.H. Plumb (ed.), *Crisis in the Humanities* (Harmondsworth, Penguin, 1964).

The Humanities beyond Interpretation

Onora O'Neill
University of Cambridge

I. Varieties of inquiry

Inquiry in the humanities has repeatedly been contrasted with inquiry in the natural sciences, often to its supposed detriment. Many nineteenth- and twentieth-century commentators claimed that the two types of inquiry use fundamentally different methods, and some of them also claimed that the approaches and results achieved by humanistic inquiry are less rigorous, less worthy, or less important than those of the natural sciences. The basic distinctions were drawn in Kant's late discussions of different types of judgement, in Schleiermacher's work on Scriptural interpretation and more broadly on hermeneutics, and in Dilthey's contrast between *Erklären* and *Verstehen*. Versions of their distinctions have shaped countless later discussions of the methods used for inquiry in the *Naturwissenschaften* (the natural sciences) and those used in the *Geisteswissenschaften* (the human sciences).

These discussions were prominent in German discussion from the early nineteenth century, and became prominent in English-language discussions from the late nineteenth century with the publication of T.H. Huxley's 1880 lecture *Science and Culture*[1] and Matthew Arnold's 1882 Rede lecture *Literature and Science*.[2] Huxley defended the approaches taken in the natural sciences and Arnold those taken in literary studies; while they disagreed in their sympathies, they were not dismissive of the methods and aims of inquiry of either sort.

However, debate became more partisan in the twentieth century. I suspect that the more strident tone in some twentieth-century writing on these themes can be ascribed to the damaging, if fortunately brief, influence of logical positivism. During the 1930s the logical positivists promoted a particularly aggressive version of empiricism, which claimed that inquiry that is neither *analytically true*[3] nor *empirically verifiable* is 'literally meaningless'. On the basis of these bald assumptions they concluded that ethics and aesthetics, theology and metaphysics, were all 'literally meaningless' and should be jettisoned.

A striking and very widely cited instance of this more partisan approach to differences between scientific and humanistic inquiry can be found in the stand-off between C.P. Snow and F.R. Leavis in the wake of Snow's 1959 Rede lecture 'The Two Cultures'.[4] One might have expected that C.P. Snow would have had interesting things to say about both scientific and humanistic inquiry. He was a physicist by training and had worked in the laboratory of the Nobel Prize-winning nuclear physicist Ernest Rutherford. He was also the author of a bestselling series of no fewer than eleven novels, *Strangers and Brothers*. In addition Snow played a leading part in recruiting scientific expertise for the British war effort. Yet his lecture on the two cultures notoriously shows little understanding of or sympathy with the methods used in humanistic inquiry, which he often dismisses as trivial or incompetent. Perhaps he had been too much influenced by Rutherford's quip that "Physics is the only real science. The rest are just stamp collecting".[5]

In his lecture on the 'two cultures' Snow affected even-handedness, but almost everything he wrote about work in the humanities, or specifically in literary studies, was hostile. He made few claims about the methods actually used by humanistic inquiry, but asserted *ad hominem* that those whom he dubs 'literary intellectuals' are "unconcerned with their brother men", "in a deep sense anti-intellectual", and are often drawn to fascism and worse. Natural scientists, he suggests, by contrast, may be ignorant – or perhaps just a little diffident! – about literature (and presumably about other areas of inquiry in the humanities), but nevertheless "they have their own culture...which contains a great deal of argument, usually much more rigorous and almost always at a much higher conceptual level than literary persons' arguments".

In Snow's account, the people he refers to as 'literary

intellectuals' engage mostly with one another and produce nothing that counts as knowledge, let alone as useful knowledge. Even more culpably, they were deeply ignorant of the exceptional scientific culture of their day, which in Cambridge included numerous Nobel Prize-winners in physics, chemistry, and medicine. Some of Snow's accounts of their ignorance of the natural sciences were not merely negative, but sneering:

> A good many times I have been present at gatherings of people who, by the standards of the traditional culture, are thought highly educated and who have with considerable gusto been expressing their incredulity at the illiteracy of scientists. Once or twice I have been provoked and have asked the company how many of them could describe the *Second Law of Thermodynamics*. The response was cold: it was also negative. Yet I was asking something which is the scientific equivalent of: *Have you read a work of Shakespeare's?*
>
> I now believe that if I had asked an even simpler question – such as, what do you mean by mass, or acceleration, which is the scientific equivalent of saying, *Can you read?* – not more than one in ten of the highly educated would have felt that I was speaking the same language. So the great edifice of modern physics goes up, and the majority of the cleverest people in the western world have about

as much insight into it as their Neolithic ancestors would have had.

In 1962 the literary critic F.R. Leavis responded to Snow's lecture in a lecture which – intentionally or otherwise – outdid Snow's sneering and critical tone. Leavis wrote "Not only is he [i.e. Snow] not a genius, he is intellectually as undistinguished as it is possible to be…'The Two Cultures' exhibits an utter lack of intellectual distinction and an embarrassing vulgarity of style".[6]

Snow was certainly *distinguished*: but not, it seems, in ways that Leavis considered worthwhile. Leavis's tone, I think, confirms the truth of Snow's assertion that disagreement and mutual disdain divided 'literary intellectuals' (and perhaps others working in the humanities) from physicists, and perhaps more generally those working in the humanities from natural scientists, at least at that time.

There are often tensions and differences between cultures, including between intellectual and academic cultures. The fault lines in the cultural and intellectual landscape at a given time may seem fundamental and unbridgeable to those who live with them. Yet I think there is no single fissure that separates the methods of inquiry used in the natural sciences from those used in the humanities. In my view, Stefan Collini was convincing when he concluded in his thoughtful introductory essay for the Canto edition of Snow's *The*

Two Cultures that, in view of the constant sprouting of sub-disciplines and interdisciplinary endeavours across the years since Snow gave his Rede lecture, "it is largely a matter of emphasis whether one regards these changes as indicating that, rather than two cultures, there are in fact two hundred and two cultures, or that there is fundamentally only one culture".[7]

II. Plurality of methods

Neither Snow nor Leavis emerged well from their stand-off. However, the deeper questions are not about the rights or wrongs of this particular bygone academic spat, but about the very project of linking areas of inquiry to methods of inquiry. As I see it, claims that there are two cultures fail for at least two distinct sets of reasons. They fail in the first place because they do not cover the possibilities: explanation and interpretation are not the only methods of inquiry. Secondly, they fail because work in any given area of inquiry, and indeed on most topics, is seldom methodologically homogeneous, and does not need to be methodologically homogeneous. I shall consider each of these reasons for doubting that the distinction between scientific and humanistic inquiry is as fundamental as Snow and Leavis, and many others, have claimed. As I see it, a very striking gap in writing that contrasts the empirical methods of scientific inquiry with the interpretive approaches of humanistic inquiry is that it ignores the importance, and all too often even the possibility, both of *formal analysis* and of *practical or normative inquiry*.

Formal methods are of great variety and importance both in scientific and in humanistic inquiry. They are central to mathematical and logical inquiry, and fundamental to inquiries in disciplines ranging from physics to musicology, from statistics to syntax. Neither scientific nor humanistic inquiry can dispense with forms of formal analysis, which are quite different from empirical, interpretive, and practical approaches to inquiry. It is notable that the logical positivists accepted that formal methods were essential, although their suggestion that these methods were reducible to analysis of 'the meaning of words' was wholly inadequate. However, I shall say no more about formal analysis here, in order to try to say something more specific about approaches to practical and normative inquiry, both in the natural sciences and in the humanities.[8]

III. Principles and judgement: directions of fit[9]

On one fundamental matter empirical and interpretive methods of inquiry are in agreement. Both see inquiry as aimed at *truth claims* about the objects studied. *Empirical inquiry* aims to make truth claims about its objects of study, and seeks to modify or retract claims that do not fit the way the world is. It is central to inquiries undertaken in daily life, in the many areas of science in which observational methods are central (e.g. experimental work; field work in domains such as botany or geology), and also in many types of work in the humanities for which empirical evidence is essential (history, archaeology, large parts of linguistics, and even of literary studies). The more theoretical areas of the natural sciences demand not merely respect for available evidence, but theoretical structures that will support predictions about the changes that will occur under specified circumstances. Testability, falsifiability, and prediction are central to inquiry in the more theoretical parts of the natural sciences, and claims found wanting by these standards are discarded.

Interpretive inquiry also aims to make truth claims about its objects of study. Like naturalistic inquiry, interpretive inquiry is directed to the way things are, rather than to changing the world. It aims to fit its claims to the world, rather than to change the world to fit its claims. It does this by seeking illuminating or revealing interpretations that *both* fit the case *and* offer further understanding or perspectives. Interpretive methods differ from empirical methods in that they do not aspire to identify unique interpretations that must replace all other proposed interpretations (though of course there is plenty of partisanship). Interpretation may be guided not only by demands for internal coherence, but also by considerations that link interpretations to specific political, religious, or other views, or that seek to link various conceptions of aesthetic, ethical, or cultural coherence with interpretive claims.

So while naturalistic and interpretive inquiry are different, both are truth-oriented. The explanatory aims of work in some in the natural sciences seek not merely to fit available evidence, but to identify and to survive the challenge of new evidence, and ideally to show that a theory covers and explains more than alternative theories, which are to be rejected. The interpretive aims of inquiry in the humanities are broader: they too seek to fit available evidence, and see interpretations as weaker if they cover less of the available evidence, or cannot accommodate some evidence. The difference is that the aim of finding an interpretation that is uniquely superior to all others is not taken either as fundamental or as indispensable.

IV. A Kantian pedigree

Distinctions between explanatory and interpretive inquiries into the way things are, and of the types of judgement that they can support, have a long pedigree. An early and still highly influential account of the distinction was proposed by Kant, who distinguished the different relationships between principles and the particular cases to which they are applied in making *determinant* and *reflective* judgements. A brief account of the distinction he drew, and of the assumptions on which it depends, supports a distinction between naturalistic and interpretive inquiry. But it does not show that these are the only approaches to inquiry – let alone that they belong to specific domains of inquiry.

Kant wrote in the *Critique of Judgement* that,

> The power of judgement in general is the faculty for thinking of the particular as contained under the universal. If the universal (the rule, the principle, the law) is given, then the power of judgment, which subsumes the particular under it…is determining [also translated *determinant*]. If, however, only the particular is given, for which the universal is to be found, then the power of judgment is merely reflecting [also translated *reflective*]. *CJ* 5:180; cf. *FI* 20:211

The distinction Kant draws is not between the items or materials to which principles are applied in the two types of judgement. Both determinant and reflective judgement take it that principles are applied to actual cases, for example, to some object, material, situation, action, text, or artefact, or to some feature of any of these. The difference between the two types of judgement rather lies in the assumptions made about principles and about the action that is taken in connecting principles and judgements. In determinant judgements the 'universal' (concept, rule, principle, or law) is presupposed or given, but in reflective judging the 'universal' (concept, rule, principle, and law) is not presupposed or given. Rather, reflective judging seeks to *find* some 'universal' for interpreting or describing a given particular. So in determinant judging, we *start* with some 'universal' (concept, rule, principle, or law) and seek to *apply* it (or them) to a case that is to hand: for example, we ask 'Is this bird a swan?', 'Is this killing a murder?', 'Is this sentence grammatically correct?' But in reflective judging we start with less: a case, but no given 'universal' (concept, rule, principle, or law). We then ask what *sort* of principle *could* or *could best* be applied to this case: 'What sort of a bird is this?'; 'What sort of an act is this?'; 'What sort of a story (or text, or artefact, or image...) is this?' Reflective judging aims to *interpret* cases or situations, actions or artefacts, objects or texts.

As Kant saw it, reflective judging is central to aesthetic judgement and purposive inquiry, and indispensable for textual interpretation, including in particular Scriptural and legal interpretation.[10] Reflective judging *embraces* indeterminacy: its aim is not to eliminate or to minimize indeterminacy, but to seek and develop illuminating (and inevitably indeterminate) ways of describing, articulating, or interpreting cases. (Of course the approaches proposed do not always strike others as illuminating: some reflective judging proposes ways of interpreting cases that are revealing or interesting, but equally some proposes interpretations that are tendentious or narrowly partisan.)

Reflective judging is therefore more open than determinant judging. This is a fundamental difference, but it builds on the fact that *both* determinant and reflective judging, *both* naturalistic inquiry and interpretive inquiry, assume that there is something – some particular object or case or situation, or aspect of an object case or situation – to be judged. In both cases judgement is truth-oriented, and seeks to fit the way things are.

V. Why practical judging is different

However, this assumption does not hold for practical or normative inquiry, which is not truth-oriented and does not seek to fit the way things are. Practical or normative judgement takes as its starting point some universal (concept, rule, principle, or law) that is to be used to *shape* the world and the natural and cultural objects it contains (in some small part), thereby producing something that *did not previously exist* and *changing the world* in some small way. In practical judgement the particular is *not given or presupposed*: it is to be *produced* by action that *fits the world to the principle*. The whole point of action-guiding practical judgement is that it has to be done *before* the particular is given: we cannot work out what to do by picking out or pointing to a particular act we shall have done at some future time. Practical judgement is directed to shaping the way things will come to be, rather than responding to the way they already are.

Practical or normative judgement is therefore distinctive in quite fundamental ways. Although it often relies on empirical assumptions, it does not aim either to *explain* features of the natural world, or to *interpret* or *articulate* aspects of objects or action, or even of culturally significant objects or action. Rather it aims to *realize, enact*, or *instantiate* certain standards or norms.[11] Since practical judgement aims to change the world, not to judge already existing aspects of the world, its *direction of fit* is the reverse of that used in determinant or in reflective judgement. Practical judgements aim to *instantiate* or *enact* principles, rather than to *apply* them to already existing cases or situations. This is why some of Kant's late discussions of practical judgement quite often (although not as systematically as would have been warranted) refer not to the *application* (*Anwendung*) of principles, but to their *enactment* or *instantiation* (*Ausübung, TP 275* or *Ausführung, TP 289*).

It may seem surprising that Kant, who wrote so much about the justification of practical principles that matter unconditionally for all action (both ethical principles and principles of justice), wrote less about practical judgement than he wrote about determinant and reflective judging. However, while he wrote more about determinant and reflective judging of cases that already exist to be judged, he turned his mind to the distinctive issues that arise in practical judgement, where the 'universal' is available but yet to be actualized, particularly in his late essay, *Theory and Practice*.[12] There he argues that practical judgement is guided not only by practical principles – some of them technical or instrumental principles, and others unconditional ethical principles and principles of justice – but also by theoretical claims.

Kant's most surprising claim in *Theory and Practice* (which I think is plausible) is that problems can arise in practical judging not because *too much* theoretical knowledge is used in making these judgements, but because *too little* is available or brought to bear. He sets aside the problem – which is real enough – that failure in judging of all sorts often arises simply because somebody has poor judgement, and considers the sorts of problems that can arise in practice even in those cases where "a natural talent [for judgement] is present" (*TP* 8:275). He argues that in such cases a "deficiency in premises" (*ibid.*) can undermine or hinder practical judgement. In making practical judgements, having more constraints, including *both* theoretical constraints *and* practical constraints, can be useful, and indeed indispensable: "it was not the fault of theory if it was of little use in practice, but rather of there having been *not enough* theory…Thus nobody can pretend to be *practically proficient* [my italics] in a science and yet scorn theory without declaring that he is an ignoramus in his field" (*TP* 8:275-6).

Rather than dismissing theoretical claims as irrelevant to practice, we should take account of those theoretical constraints that can be used in shaping the world to fit the relevant practical principles, so ensuring that *taken together* practical principles and theoretical constraints can shape action that is to meet the demands of technical expertise or of duty (or both) with adequate specificity in actual circumstances. Depending on the context, theoretical constraints make it possible to bring multiple considerations to bear on making a practical judgement. Where it is feasible to draw on a range of theoretical knowledge it may be possible to reach clearer views about (for example) the *availability*, the *feasibility*, the *effectiveness*, the *affordability*, or the *social acceptability* of specific ways of meeting technical or moral requirements in actual situations. Theoretical considerations are indispensable in shaping the way in which normative principles are to be enacted or respected.

VI. Practical judgement: technical constraints

So, as Kant sees it, "more theory" can be indispensable for making both technical or professional judgements, and moral judgements. Technical experts, who aim to put their expertise into practice in pursuing *desired* or *required* ends, can be helped to identify how this might best be done in a given situation by drawing on a sufficient range of theoretical considerations that bear on the likely feasibility, the likely effects of action to be taken, the likely 'side' effects of a given approach, and many other considerations that can bear on ways of enacting principles in actual situations. In prescribing medical treatment it is useful to know quite a lot about the aetiology and transmission of the condition to be treated, and about the differing effects of specific treatments. In firing an artillery piece it is useful to know not only about ballistics, but about other constraints that may affect the accuracy of a shot, such as those that can be supplied by theoretical accounts of wind speed, air pressure, or friction (both of these are Kant's examples).

The claim that technical practice can fail even *where agents have good capacities for judgement*, because there is 'not enough' (or not good enough) theory is plausible enough. Physicians who lack an adequate theory of infection; architects who do not know enough about the properties of the building materials they propose to use; farmers who lack an understanding of the effects of local growing conditions on the growth of the seedlings they plan to plant – all may go wrong in practice, *even if their capacities for judgement are good*. In such cases Kant's claim that practice can fail because expertise is limited by lack of theory makes good sense. *Practical* judgement on his account needs to draw on *many* sorts of theoretical claims, and not only – as is sometimes imagined – on means–ends connections. It also needs to find ways of enacting the relevant practical principles that take adequate account of many specific features of the actual situations.

VII. Practical judgement and moral constraints

Realism about these and other constraints is also needed in working out how the demands of morality are to be met in actual situations. Ethical judgement does not aim to fit the world as it is, but to change the world to fit certain moral principles, and this can be done only by taking account of a wide range of theoretical constraints that bear on the enactment of principles under varied conditions.

This picture of practical judgement in ethics and politics is reiterated in Kant's political writings, where he takes a principled view of justice, yet is always a political realist, and cautions against the imprudent or unrealistic pursuit of moral aims in political practice. For Kant a commitment to justice is not adequate unless combined with a realistic grip on the ways in which the world can and cannot be changed, and of the theoretical and empirical constraints that are relevant to shaping action.

So as Kant sees it, unconditional, *morally practical* theories indeed differ from *technically practical* theories. But both technical and moral judgement need to take realistic account of multiple constraints, and hence of the evidence that can be obtained from those bodies of theoretical knowledge that offer useful accounts of these constraints. Morally practical judgement, like expert and technical judgement, needs to take account not merely of means–ends relations, but of a wide range of constraints and prudential considerations that bear on the prospects of enacting principles in actual situations.

VIII. Methodological pluralism within domains of inquiry

Seeking to confine the methods used in domains of inquiry to theoretical explanation (for scientific and other empirical inquiry) and interpretive understanding (for inquiry in the humanities) over-simplifies, indeed distorts, the ways in which inquiry not merely *may*, but *must* be structured. This simplification has two aspects. The first defect is that both positions overlook the importance both of formal methods and of practical or normative methods for all inquiry, and for activity that seeks either to change the world, or to make truth-claims about aspects of the world. The second and broader defect, on which I shall comment very briefly, is the mistaken assumption that there is or should be a systematic link between domains of inquiry and methods of inquiry.

A simplistic contrast between the methods of the natural sciences and the humanities offers not merely an impoverished, but an inaccurate map of inquiry in many fields. There are more things that matter in working out how to inquire about countless matters than can be found in any 'two cultures' view of available or acceptable methods. There is no need, and no prospect, of aligning areas or domains of inquiry one-to-one with methods of inquiry. Indeed, for many good reasons, what goes on in most areas of inquiry is unavoidably and deeply methodologically plural.

Of course, it is true that work in the experimental sciences rightly pays a lot of attention to empirical evidence and experimental design. But it also frequently relies on interpretation, and sometimes on normative reasoning. This is not new. When Kant distinguished determinant from interpretive judgement, he accepted that scientific inquiry also uses some interpretive approaches and even allowed that (while there can be no 'science of beauty') scientific theories can, for example, be beautiful.[13]

And, perhaps more surprisingly, it is also abundantly clear that scientific inquiry uses normative reasoning. Uncontroversially, instrumental reasoning is constantly used in the application of science, but wider forms of normative reasoning are used and indeed are necessary in reaching decisions about scientific norms, standards, and metrics. A striking and very recent instance of normative reasoning in scientific inquiry was the decision of the *General Conference on Weights and Measures*, which met in November 2018 in Versailles, to redefine the kilogram in terms of the Planck constant, rather than (as has previously been the case) by reference to a paradigmatic physical object (which inevitably varies in minute ways across time). Analogous redefinitions have been agreed for other basic physical units.

And just as interpretive and normative reasoning are indispensable for scientific inquiry, empirical reasoning is indispensable for a great deal of inquiry in the humanities. Anyone working in history or archaeology or linguistics who suggested that discovering, assembling, checking, and recording empirical evidence accurately is irrelevant in their discipline would rightly meet short shrift.

IX. Inquiring right

Neither the temptation to think that each field must use one and only one method of inquiry nor the contrary claim that this is implausible is new. In his *Doctrine of Method* Descartes asserted that reason is "whole and complete in each of us", and that there is a "*Method of rightly Conducting One's Reason and Seeking the Truth in the Sciences*".[14] Yet a few years earlier the poet John Donne had made the contrary claim, insisting on the inherent complexity of inquiry. In his Third Satire, written in the 1590s, Donne describes the strenuous task of seeking religious truth, and insists that here too there is no single method:

> To stand inquiring right, is not to stray;
> To sleep, or run wrong, is. On a huge hill,
> Cragged and steep, Truth stands, and he that will
> Reach her, about must and about must go,
> And what the hill's suddenness resists, win so.

Donne compares the task of seeking the truth to climbing a steep hill, where those who inquire repeatedly find that they "about must and about must go", retracing, revising, and testing earlier thoughts and claims. This, it seems to me, is probably a better account of what is needed in seeking to guide belief or action, not only in religious matters, but in the natural sciences and the humanities. There is no single or simple method either for discovering what is true, or for deciding what to do. Both truth-oriented and practical inquiry must respect multiple norms and standards, and may need repeated efforts to advance and correct initial endeavours.

The pluralism of methods of inquiry is in many ways an everyday and widely accepted matter. The neglect of formal and of practical or normative questions in discussions of scientific and humanistic inquiry is not repeated in the actual organization either of universities and academies, or of corporate or government research departments or thinktanks, or in the varieties of inquiry that they undertake. Many university departments and research institutions focus at least in part on *practical* and *policy* questions and the *normative* reasoning that they require (whether they do so with sufficient rigour is a further matter). Faculties of science, technology, and engineering often investigate technical norms and their practical implementation. Faculties of philosophy and law investigate ethical, political, and legal norms and seek to address questions not only about their justification, and their fitness for purpose, but about their implementation. A lot of social inquiry addresses policy questions. Government and corporate research departments, and many think tanks, investigate practical questions about public policy and technical decisions.

In short, a contrast between naturalistic and interpretive inquiry may or may not be illuminating, but it is neither exhaustive, nor reflected in the actual organization of practices of inquiry. All the more reason, then, to think broadly about differing types of inquiry, about the full range of standards that they need to meet, and about the connections between methods of inquiry in differing areas of inquiry.

It is not feasible to exclude practical judgement from work either in the humanities or in the natural sciences. While the fantasy that science is or should be 'value neutral' lingers in some quarters, the standards and practical judgements made in undertaking scientific research also require scrutiny and vindication. As we have seen, there is plenty of normative reasoning in scientific work, ranging from discussions about choices of metrics and classifications, to consideration of the epistemic and ethical norms that adequate research requires. Equally there is plenty of empirical and normative reasoning in work in the humanities, despite occasional misplaced expressions of enthusiasm for claims that interpretation is all. And there is plenty of awareness among those who avowedly address practical issues, whether in ethics or in engineering, that practical principles do not stand alone and that it is important to take a realistic view of empirical constraints on their implementation. So I conclude that there is no point, and no need, to redraw our conventional maps of the academic world. However, it would be helpful to be much more explicit about the diversity of methods of inquiry that are often needed for work both in the humanities and in the natural sciences, and to set aside assumptions that distinctive areas of inquiry have entirely distinctive methods of inquiry.

References

1. T.H. Huxley, *Science and Culture*, 1880, reprinted in his *Science and Education: Essays* (London, 1893), pp.134-59. Huxley had delivered a Rede Lecture on a different theme in 1883.
2. M. Arnold, 'Literature and Science', in R.H. Super (ed.), *The Complete Prose Works of Matthew Arnold*, vol. X (Ann Arbor: University of Michigan Press, 1974), pp.52-73.
3. The logical positivists relied on a hazy view of analyticity, which they glossed simply as 'true in virtue of the meaning of words'. For this they were soon taken to task, in particular by W.V.O. Quine in 'Two Dogmas of Empiricism', *The Philosophical Review, 60:1 (1951), pp.20-43;* doi:10.2307/2181906; reprinted in W.V.O. Quine, *From a Logical Point of View* (Cambridge, MA: Harvard University Press, 1953). Quine did not adopt Kant's more precise but narrow view of analyticity, and relied on a version of pragmatism.
4. C.P Snow, *The Two Cultures* (1959); Canto edition with introduction by Stefan Collini, Cambridge: Cambridge University Press, 1998. Page references are to this edition. Snow's lecture was the hundredth lecture in the modern series of Rede Lec-

tures as one-off lectures; in their older version the Rede Lectures date back to the sixteenth century.
5   A number of versions of this comment are in circulation, but there appears to be no textual source.
6   Leavis's response was published in *The Spectator* on 9 March 1962, and later (after legal vetting) in book form.
7   Stefan Collini, Introductory essay to *The Two Cultures*, p.xliv.
8   See Rens Bod, *A New History of the Humanities: the Search for Principles and Patterns from Antiquity to the Present* (Oxford: Oxford Univesity Press, 2016), which emphasizes the roles of pattern, structure, and form for work in the humanities.
9   For the term 'direction of fit' see J.L. Austin, *How to Do Things with Words: The William James Lectures Delivered at Harvard University in 1955* (Oxford: Oxford University Press, 1962) and G.E.M. Anscombe, *Intention* (Oxford: Blackwell, 1957). However, the distinction is older.
10 Kant's late work includes extensive discussion of textual interpretation, and specifically of Scriptural and legal interpretation. See *Religion within the Boundaries of Mere Reason* [1793], tr. George di Giovanni, in Immanuel Kant, *Religion and Rational Theology*, ed. Allen W. Wood and George di Giovanni (Cambridge: Cambridge University Press, 1996) and *The Conflict of the Faculties* [1798], tr. Mary J. Gregor and Robert Anchor, in Immanuel Kant, *Religion and Rational Theology*, ed. Allen W. Wood and George di Giovanni (Cambridge: Cambridge University Press, 1996). These discussions are quite different from those in which he addresses practical judgement; see next section.
11 Some writers, often those with Aristotelian or Wittgensteinian views of ethics, have tried to construe moral judgements as interpretive, by seeing them as a matter of *appraising* or *appreciating* actual or hypothetical situations. The approach has been criticized for aestheticizing ethics. But its deeper shortcoming is that acts that have not yet been done are not available to be appraised or appreciated. I explore this in more detail in 'Modern Moral Philosophy and the Problem of Relevant Descriptions', in Onora O'Neill, *From Principles to Practice: Normativity and Judgement in Ethics and Politics* (Cambridge: Cambridge University Press, 2018), pp.11-25.

12 Immanuel Kant, *On the Common Saying: That may be correct in theory, but it is of no use in practice* [*TP*] [1793], tr. Mary J. Gregor, in *Kant's Practical Philosophy* (Cambridge: Cambridge University Press, 1996).

13 See Rudolf Makkreel, *Orientation and Judgment in Hermeneutics* (Chicago: University of Chicago Press, 2015); Angela Breitenbach, 'The Beauty of Science without the Science of Beauty: Kant and the Rationalists on the Aesthetics of Cognition', *Journal of the History of Philosophy*, 56:2(2018), pp.281-304.

14 René Descartes, *Discourse on the method of rightly Conducting One's Reason and Seeking the Truth in the Sciences* [1637], in Philosophical *Writings of Descartes*, vol. I, tr. John Cottingham, Robert Stoothof, and Dugald Murdoch (Cambridge: Cambridge University Press, 1985).

How the Humanities Have Changed the World

Rens Bod
University of Amsterdam[1]

Introduction

There is a preconception so deeply rooted in our culture that even scholars seem to believe it. This is the assumption that whatever the humanities do, they do not solve concrete problems, let alone result in technological applications.[2] Yet a quick glance at the general history of the humanities[3] shows otherwise: contrary to common wisdom, insights and methods from the humanities solved concrete problems and resulted in applications that had a profound impact on science and technology. To be sure, such utilizations of humanistic insights and methods sometimes emerged after considerable time. But methods and theories from the humanities have been picked up and used in a wide variety of other disciplines.

In the following I will review some of the far-reaching effects of humanistic inquiry and discuss their influence on science and technology. It is surprising that overviews of the history of science have left out the impact received from the humanities.[4] This essay opts for an inclusive history of knowledge where the sciences and the humanities are discussed on a par.[5] In fact I will argue that the history of science cannot be properly understood without taking into account the history of the humanities (and vice versa).

There is a question of what we mean by the 'humanities'. While we usually know what is meant by the 'sciences', we are left empty-handed when asked for a definition of the humanities (see Stefan Collini's essay in this volume for a discussion of the term). As a working definition for this essay, I shall refer to the humanities as "the disciplines that investigate the products of the human mind".[6] Thus disciplines like linguistics, art history, literary studies, musicology, theatre studies, history, and philology are all humanistic disciplines, as well as many others.

I. Linguistics and the impact of grammar

One of the most salient technological developments during the last century has been the emergence of information technology. While this development is not usually seen as a product of the humanities, it was a humanistic discipline – the study of language – that made information technology possible. A fundamental insight in linguistics is that language can be described by a system of rules, known as a *grammar*. The concept of grammar is older than the first systematic Greek descriptions of language. The first extant grammar is found in the work *Ashtadhyayi* (Eight Books) by the Indian grammarian Panini,[7] who lived around 500 BCE.[8] The *Ashtadhyayi* contains one of the most complete grammars in existence.[9] Panini developed a set of 3,959 rules that covers all possible sentences in Sanskrit. That is, Panini's grammar can determine whether a given sequence of sounds is a correctly formed sentence in Sanskrit. Panini's grammar is still unsurpassed.[10] After two and a half thousand years, the efficacy of this system of nearly four thousand complex interconnected rules remains undisputed.

Panini was not just a descriptive linguist, however; the underlying formalism he developed is just as interesting. To write down his 3,959 rules, he used a grammatical system that is nowadays known as *rewrite grammar*.[11] His rewrite grammar consists of rules that indicate how a certain part of a sentence (a 'phrase') can be built up ('rewritten') out of other, smaller phrases and words, provided they appear in a certain combination. In fact not every combination of words or phrases leads to a grammatical sentence. For example, in English there is a rule that states that a nominal phrase can consist of an article and a noun, as in 'the house'. Clearly, these words only form a correct phrase if the article appears before the noun.

Panini's approach in the *Ashtadhyayi* was to make his grammar system explicit and comprehensive. He devised a set of rules that, using a combination of a finite number of lexical units (the *word stems*), could cover all correct Sanskrit utterances.[12] Panini invented an ordered system of rules in order to achieve this goal. His rules are applied in a certain order so as to arrive at a linguistic utterance. This corresponds to the concept of an algorithm: a procedure that generates a result in a finite number of sequential steps. Panini's rules are also *optional*,[13] which means there is always more than one possible choice (otherwise it would only be possible to cover one linguistic utterance). He introduced a metarule in order to make his system consistent: "If two rules conflict, the last rule prevails".[14] Panini organized his grammar so that this metarule is always valid.

One of the other influential ideas in Panini's system of rules is that a grammar rule can invoke itself – a given construction can contain another example of that construction. This is known as recursion, in Sanskrit known as *Nyāya*. Recursion occurs for example in the English sentence, 'He was harassed by the individual who was caught by the policeman who was spotted by the photographer'. We can make this sentence longer, indeed as long as we want, by recursively applying the grammatical rule for subordinate clauses in English (and by choosing different words from the lexicon). The use of recursion allowed Panini to describe the unlimited number of Sanskrit sentences with a finite number of rules.

The invention of a precise system of grammar rules together with the concept of recursion makes Panini the most original linguist of antiquity. His grammar is regarded as a major monument in human thought.[15] Only towards the end of the eighteenth century was Panini's grammar discovered by European scholars, and it took another century and a half before it was relatively well understood. In the 1950s, the renowned linguist Noam Chomsky based his work on Panini's ideas and called him his spiritual father.[16] Yet it is still an open question whether a finite system of rules can represent a 'complete' grammar of a living language[17] – only for a dead language like Sanskrit does this seem to be beyond doubt.

Nevertheless, the notion of grammar appeared to be exceptionally well suited for describing – and creating – a rather different kind of language: high-level programming languages for computers. In contrast with low-level programming languages, high-level programming languages do not use zeroes and ones or other machine-like codes for programming. Instead they use statements that resemble sentences and phrases in human languages, including recursive structures (which are only in a second stage translated into the underlying machine language and finally into zeroes and ones by a separate algorithm). It was Panini's formalism of grammar with recursion that came to be applied by John Backus to design the full syntax of the first high-level programming language *ALGOL60*. The resulting formalism is also referred to as the Panini-Backus form.[18] Virtually all current high-level programming languages are written in a formalism that incorporates the linguistic notion of a grammar with recursion.[19] Such a grammar determines whether a given sequence of statements forms a correct expression in a particular programming language. If the statements follow the rules of the grammar, they are correct, which means that they can be processed by the underlying machine language.

The linguistic formalism of rewrite grammar was taken over and reused by computer scientists, giving the field of computer science and information technology an unprecedented impulse. In the history of computer science, the linguistic invention of a rewrite grammar plays a key role.[20]

II. Philology and the biological appropriation of text reconstruction techniques

Concepts and methods from the language sciences also found their way in the life sciences. In the course of the 1950s, biologists came to represent organisms and molecules as information systems by using linguistic tropes and textual analogies.[21] The human genome was viewed as a textual information system: the ways DNA sequences could be replicated, mutated, and contaminated were phrased in terms of philological and computational concepts. These representations of heredity did not arise from the inner logic of DNA genetics. Instead, they had been transported into molecular biology from cybernetics, information theory, and computer science,[22] which in turn had imported these metaphors from the language sciences, as discussed above.[23] But while computer scientists had looked mainly at linguistics, molecular biologists (also) looked at stemmatic philology – the theory of text reconstruction that creates a tree of variants (a stemma) of the transmission of a text so as to deduce its presumed archetype.

The way biologists made use of textual concepts in DNA genetics was not just a matter of metaphor or analogy. If we look at the deeper level of formalisms used in philology and DNA genetics, we can discern an equivalence between nineteenth-century stemmatic philology and twentieth-century molecular biology. This equivalence went even further than that between linguistics and computer science: not only was the formalism of a philological tree of texts (or stemma) taken over by biologists, but also several of the rules or operations that philologists had developed to operate on a stemma.

The history of the notion of stemma has been investigated in various places. Robert O'Hara draws attention to the presence of "trees of history" glossed as "branching diagrams of genealogical descent and change" in a wide variety of disciplines: textual criticism, evolutionary biology, historical linguistics, and information science.[24] The first ever stemma seems to have been produced for Swedish legal manuscripts by Carl Johan Schlyter in 1827.[25] It predates the use of the first genealogical trees in linguistics by August Schleicher in 1850 and evolutionary biology by Charles Darwin in 1859. It was the philologist Karl Lachmann (1793-1851) who in 1850 spelled out the rules that applied to a philological stemma of texts and how they could be used in reconstructing the original text from hereditary copies in the family tree.[26] While the origins of this technique of text reconstruction are much older – it can be traced back to the early humanists, in particular to Angelo Poliziano[27] – only in the nineteenth century was this humanistic practice turned into a more or less orderly set of rules. These rules were further refined and mathematically formalized in the early twentieth century,[28] which resulted in several formal rules or operations for describing the 'errors' in variants due to copying mistakes, such as rules for *substitution*, *deletion*, and *insertion* of elements.[29]

These operations of substitution, insertion, and deletion turned out to be applicable both to sequences of lexical elements and to sequences of DNA elements – thus independent of whether these elements were due to *scribal alterations* arising over successive generations of recopied manuscripts or to *genetic mutations* in DNA molecules occurring through successive generations.[30] At the level of the formalism used and (several of the) operations applied, there is not just analogy but equivalence between philology and genetics![31] That is, both in philology and genetics a sequence (be they words in the case of a manuscript, or nucleotides in the case of DNA) is copied on the basis of the same operations. When changes occur, textual changes and DNA mutations are described by the same system of rules or operations. For example, the operation of substitution of one word for another (in text copying) is equal to the substitution of a nucleotide for another (in DNA copying). The elements differ, but the abstract rule or operation is the same. And the operation of insertion or deletion of words is formally equal to the rule of insertion and deletion of nucleotides. Even philological contamination, whereby pieces from several manuscripts are combined, follows the same formal rule in DNA genetics, known as genetic recombination.[32]

Thus the formalism and rule system from the discipline of textual philology were decontextualized and then recontextualized in the new field of genetics. We cannot really grasp the history of science, in this case twentieth-century genetics, if we neglect the long-term history of its methods, some of which originate in the humanities, in this case nineteenth-century stemmatic philology. But the opposite also holds. In fact, the story does not finish here. Over the last few decades, stemmatics in biology has led to the new field of *cladistics*, which has turned into a highly sophisticated computer-assisted methodology for creating history trees in biology. Although originating in philology, cladistics has now influenced philology and historical linguistics again, not only technically but also conceptually.[33] Cladistic software is currently applied to stemmatic philology to derive highly sophisticated trees of texts that lead to new questions in philology.[34] Thus the interaction between humanistic and scientific disciplines is a highly dynamic one; it is rarely a one-way transfer: formalisms and rule systems from philology first entered biology and subsequently came back to philology in computational form. The same happened with linguistics and computer science: the linguistic notion of grammar was first transferred to computer science, from which the notion of computational grammar came back to linguistics, leading to the field of computational linguistics.

III. The effectiveness of historical source criticism

One might object that linguistics and stemmatic philology, with their formalized methods, do belong to the sciences rather than to the humanities – and it is the historical disciplines that are the real backbone of humanistic research. Historiography, as the German philosopher Wilhelm Dilthey put it, is not concerned with explaining events but with understanding them, as illustrated by the German word *verstehen*.[35] In the view of the Neo-Kantians, rather than aiming at finding general rules or regularities (nomothetic), as linguistics and stemmatic philology do, historiography focuses on the specific (idiographic).[36] Yet it is also the discipline of historiography that developed the general and widely applicable method of *source criticism*. This method is used not only in historical research but also in other disciplines for critically evaluating sources especially in forensic science, evidence-based medicine, and jurisprudence.[37] It is, for instance, used at the International Court of Justice and at the International Criminal Court to determine whether a source is authentic or whether it has been forged.

The notion of source criticism itself has a notable history. It can already be found in Herodotus, who compared contradicting sources in terms of plausibility.[38] It developed via Thucydides, who only accepted sources based on eyewitness accounts,[39] and Polybius, who stressed personal experience as the most reliable source,[40] into the more textual approach to historical source criticism that we find in the Roman republic and onwards, where written sources were regarded as the most reliable.[41] Unlike oral sources, written sources guaranteed some level of verifiability, but the problem of contradictory sources remained, and thus factors such as the authority of a written source played a fundamental role in determining whether to accept it as a reliable witness.

Usually, the nineteenth-century historian Leopold von Ranke (1795-1886) is credited with the invention of a systematic source criticism that aims to determine whether a document corresponds to historical reality.[42] Both the content of the source and its external facets, such as the form and the carrier, were subjected to a critical analysis. But a very similar kind of source criticism had already been practiced several centuries before, first by early humanists, and later during the heyday of humanist historiography in the sixteenth and seventeenth centuries. One of the most illustrious examples of early source criticism is Lorenzo Valla's famous rebuttal of the document known as the *Donatio Constantini* in 1440.[43] As is well known, the *Donatio* stated that the emperor Constantine had transferred authority over the Western Roman empire to Pope Sylvester I. It gave a justification for the church's worldly power. Although others had suggested earlier that the document was a forgery,[44] it was Valla who convincingly showed that the document could not have been written in the fourth century during the reign of Constantine. By combining the methods of historical, lexical, and logical criticism, Valla showed that a number of events, words, and phrases in the document were of medieval origin and that part of the discourse was in fact logically inconsistent. Valla's demonstration was so convincing that it was immediately accepted – even (initially) by the pope – until it was used by reformers like Martin Luther in their arguments against the church, and then placed on the Index.[45]

While Valla's impact was impressive, source criticism probably had its greatest impact on early modern thought through the work of Joseph Scaliger (1540-1609), who was active at the University of Leiden in the late sixteenth and early seventeenth centuries.[46] Scaliger aimed at unifying all ancient histories (Graeco-Roman, Babylonian, Egyptian, Persian, and Jewish) so as to create the definitive historical chronology from the earliest era to his own time.[47] In doing so, he not only had to compare many different calendar systems but a very large number of historical sources too. Scaliger therefore critically compared various historical texts, among them Manetho's list of Egyptian dynasties. Using the information from these sources, particularly about the duration of the different dynasties, he was able to date the beginning of the first Egyptian dynasty to 5285 BCE. To his dismay this date was nearly 1,300 years before the generally accepted day of Creation, which according to biblical chronology had to be around 4000 BCE. However, Scaliger did not draw the ultimate conclusion from his discovery, which would have meant that either the Bible or his own method was wrong. In order to 'save the phenomena', Scaliger introduced a new time pattern – the *tempus prolepticon* – a time before time.[48] He placed every event that occurred before the Creation, such as the early Egyptian kings, in this proleptic time. Clearly, for a Protestant in around 1600 it was inconceivable to cast doubt on the Bible. Yet Scaliger was too consistent to give up on his critical method so readily.

Scaliger's discovery, however, appeared to be a time bomb. Only a couple of generations later, an increasing number of scholars – from Isaac Vossius to Spinoza –

realized that the only possible interpretation of Scaliger's result was that the earliest Egyptian kings had actually lived before the biblical date of the Creation. This meant that the Bible could not be taken seriously as a historical source. Scaliger's pattern of world history conflicted with biblical chronology, and this triggered a chain of biblical criticism that resulted in the early Enlightenment.[49]

IV. The influence and impact of other humanistic discoveries

The examples of the impact of the humanities on science and technology discussed so far are by no means exhaustive. A fuller account should certainly also mention Leon Battista Alberti's work *De pictura* (1435), which provided the first theoretical description and analysis of linear perspective. Alberti developed a completely articulated method for the illusionistic reproduction of three-dimensional objects on a two-dimensional surface (the discovery of which he attributes to the sculptor and architect Filippo Brunelleschi). This method and its impact on painting literally changed our view of the world. It led not only to a revolution in European painting and art theory, but also to entirely new design techniques in architecture that were inconceivable without the use of linear perspective.[50]

Neither should an overview of the impact of the

humanities on the sciences overlook the exploration of musical dissonance and consonance by early humanists. The humanistic study of harmony revealed the synergetic interaction between theory and empiricism, which was passed on to the 'new scientists' of the seventeenth century, who elaborated it again in their own way.[51] This has in particular been studied in the relation between Vincenzo Galilei and his son Galileo Galilei. Vincenzo was a humanist, composer, and music theoretician who performed, among other things, experiments with the monochord. He experimented with strings of different lengths, materials, and tensions, and aimed to refute some of the most influential musical theorists of his day (Gioseffo Zarlino) not just by theoretical considerations but by experiment. Galileo seems to have applied his father's empirical methodology to his own experiments with balls rolled down an inclined plane. This intricate connection between music and nature was not new, as music theory had been treated as a matter of cosmological importance ever since Pythagoras.[52] What *was* new, however, was that the humanists employed a strongly empirical method for the study of their subject matter (music, but also texts), in which empiricism was to have the last word, no matter how fine the underlying theory was. In doing so these early humanists created – or should we say, 'discovered' – the synergy between theory and empiricism. They did so well before the 'new scientists' of the seventeenth century applied the empirical approach to the study of nature and brought it to great heights.[53]

The examples given so far are the tip of the iceberg. We can remind ourselves how the nineteenth-century discovery of the Indo-European language family – which at the time was called 'comparative philology' – defined our view of the relationships between peoples, for better and worse. Among other things, this discovery gave a boost to scientific racism, in particular to the hypothesis of the existence of a 'pure' Aryan race, a theory that would be taken over much later by the National Socialists.[54] This shows that the impact of the humanities is not necessarily positive. The claim that the humanities are essential to a critical mentality and democracy (as Martha Nussbaum contends[55]) may deserve a more nuanced discussion.[56] For nineteenth-century scholars like Friedrich Max Müller and Christian Lassen, it was straightforward that the linguistic evidence for an ur-language meant that there was a pure Aryan race and that some other races were endlessly mixed and impure.[57] Some of the most critical linguists and philosophers of the time accepted this view. If we want to describe the history of scientific racism, we cannot leave out the history of comparative philology.

We should also add some examples from the more recent humanities disciplines such as film studies and television studies. In film studies, for example, scholars have developed methods of analyzing film by integrating insights from semiology, literary studies, and linguistics. We see this most clearly in the work of Christian Metz (1931-1993), who developed his "Grande Syntagmatique" in which he called the building blocks of film *syntagmas*. In the spirit of Noam Chomsky's generative syntax,[58] Metz designed a number of theoretical principles to create a hierarchical organization for these syntagmas so that the cinematic

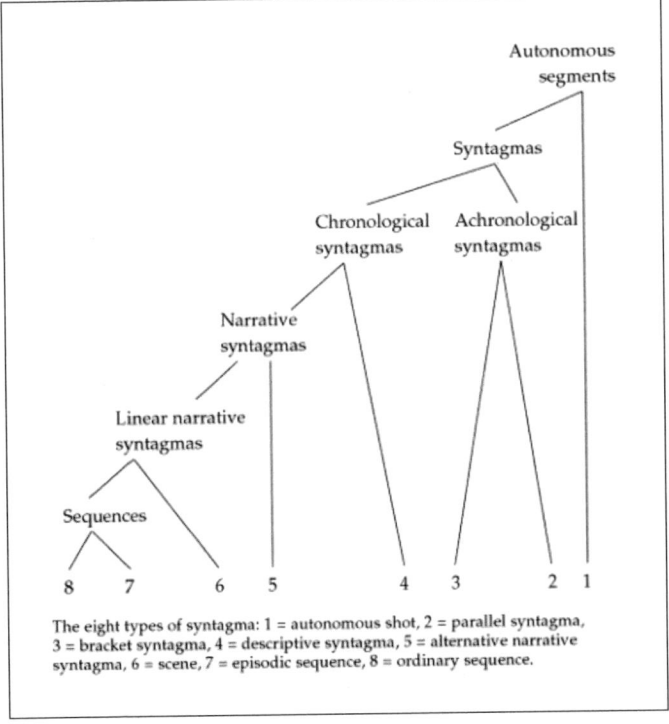

Figure 1. Christian Metz's "Grande Syntagmatique".
From: Warren Buckland, *The Cognitive Semiotics of Film* (Cambridge: Cambridge University Press, 2000), p.115.

structure of the film as a whole could be visualized and interpreted. Such a cinematic narrative structure is represented by a tree diagram where the leaves of the tree represent film scenes and the branched structure reflects the relationships between the scenes (see Figure 1).

This formal analysis into building blocks has led to some surprising results. For example, the narrative structure of the popular television series *CSI: Crime Scene Investigation*, which has run for years, has been found to consist of only eight narrative building blocks that are endlessly reshuffled.[59]

Another important insight from the analysis of the medium of television indicates that viewers are captured through 'flows' – i.e. non-stop streams of information, advertising, entertainment, and trailers – whose purpose is to keep the viewer tuned to a particular channel.[60] Time will tell whether these insights and discoveries will have applications in science or technology, but they are in any event sensational.

My review of the history of the impact of the humanities has only scratched the surface, but it has made clear that insights from the humanities have had a profound influence on science, technology, and society. The humanities gave us grammar formalisms (linguistics) that were used in the development of high-level programming languages. The humanities provided tools for text reconstruction (stemmatic philology) that could be applied to DNA analysis. They also developed widely applicable source-critical methods (historiography) which are used in a variety of fields, from forensics to medicine. And the humanities most probably invented the empirical cycle of research, where empiricism gets the last word no matter how beautiful the theory may be (early humanism). A thorough understanding of the development of systematic knowledge must therefore include both (the histories of) the humanities and the sciences. To do so, we must put aside our preconceptions of humanistic and scientific endeavours, and study the scholarly and scientific texts, practices, and methods from the past anew.[61]

References

1 This essay is partly based on my Academy Lecture delivered at the Norwegian Academy of Science and Letters in 2016, and partly on my talk delivered at the Carlsberg Foundation in 2018. I greatly thank both the Norwegian Academy and The Carlsberg Foundation for their hospitality and for making these meetings possible.
2 Examples of this preconception can be found in almost any discussion of the humanities, including Martha Nussbaum, *Not for Profit: Why Democracy Needs the Humanities* (Princeton, NJ: Princeton University Press, 2010); Jörg-Dieter Gauger and Günther Rüther (eds), *Warum die Geisteswissenschaften Zukunft haben!* (Basel: Herder, 2007); Stanley Fish, "Will the Humanities Save Us?", *New York Times*, 6 January 2008; Jonathan Bate (ed.), *The Public Value of the Humanities* (London: Bloomsbury Academic, 2010). For a historical overview, see Helen Small, *The Value of the Humanities* (Oxford: Oxford University Press, 2013).

3   See e.g. Rens Bod, *A New History of the Humanities: The Search for Principles and Patterns from Antiquity to the Present* (Oxford: Oxford University Press, 2013); James Turner, *Philology: The Hidden Origins of the Modern Humanities* (Princeton, NJ: Princeton University Press, 2014). See also the three edited volumes on the comparative history of the humanities: R. Bod, J. Maat and T. Weststeijn (eds), *The Making of the Humanities, Vol. I: Early Modern Europe* (Amsterdam: Amsterdam University Press, 2010); R. Bod, J. Maat and T. Weststeijn (eds), *The Making of the Humanities, Vol. II: From Early Modern to Modern Disciplines* (Amsterdam: Amsterdam University Press, 2012); R. Bod, J. Maat and T. Weststeijn (eds), *The Making of the Humanities, Vol. III: The Modern Humanities* (Amsterdam: Amsterdam University Press, 2014).

4   This is not the place to summarize the historiography of science, but overviews of the history of science are as old as the field itself and continue to be written. They include William Whewell, *History of the Inductive Sciences*, 3 volumes (Cambridge: Parker, 1837); George Sarton, *Introduction to the History of Science*, 3 volumes (Baltimore: Williams and Wilkins, 1931-1947); Stephen Mason, *A History of the Sciences* (New York: Macmillan, 1962); William Dampier, *A History of Science and Its Relation to Philosophy and Religion* (Cambridge: Cambridge University Press, 1966); James McClellan and Harold Dorn, *Science and Technology in World History* (Baltimore: Johns Hopkins University Press, 1999); Frederick Gregory, *Natural Science in Western History* (Belmont, CA: Wadsworth Publishing, 2007); Patricia Fara, *Science: A Four Thousand Year History* (Oxford: Oxford University Press, 2009).

5   See Rens Bod, *Een Wereld Vol Patronen: De Geschiedenis van Kennis* ["A World of Patterns: The History of Knowledge"] (Amsterdam: Prometheus, 2019); in Dutch, to appear in English in 2021.

6   Wilhelm Dilthey, *Einleitung in die Geisteswissenschaften: Versuch einer Grundlegung für das Studium der Gesellschaft und der Geschichte* (Leipzig: Duncker & Humblot, 1883), pp.11ff. For an English translation, see Wilhelm Dilthey, *Selected*

Works, vol. I, tr. and ed. Rudolf Makkreel and Frithjof Rodi (Princeton, NJ. Princeton University Press, 1991).

7   The transcription from Sanskrit by Indologists is usually 'Pāṇini', where the accent is on the first syllable ('Pā'). For this essay I will use the more common transcription 'Panini'.

8   Paul Kiparsky, 'Paninian Linguistics', in *The Encyclopedia of Language and Linguistics* (Amsterdam: Elsevier, 1993).

9   For an accessible translation of the *Ashtadhyayi*, with examples and commentaries, see Panini, *The Ashtadhyayi – Translated into English by Srisa Chandra Vasu* (1923; repr., Charleston: Nabu Press 2011).

10 Esa Itkonen, *Universal History of Linguistics* (Amsterdam and Philadelphia: Benjamins, 1991), p.12ff.

11 Frits Staal, *Universals: Studies in Indian Logic and Linguistics* (Chicago: University of Chicago Press, 1988), p.3.

12 Vidyaniwas Misra, *The Descriptive Technique of Panini: An Introduction* (The Hague: Mouton, 1966), pp.43ff.

13 Panini's rule 2.1.11 (*vibhasa*) in the *Ashtadhyayi*.

14 Panini's rule 1.4.2 in the *Ashtadhyayi*.

15 Leonard Bloomfield, *Language* (1933; repr., Chicago: University of Chicago Press, 1984), p.11.

16 For a discussion of the relation between Panini and Chomsky, see Bod, *A New History of the Humanities*, pp.290-95.

17 See Rens Bod, *Beyond Grammar* (Chicago: University of Chicago Press, 1998).

18 P.Z. Ingerman, 'Panini-Backus Form Suggested', *Communications of the ACM*, 10:3 (1967), p.137.

19 See Erol Gelenbe and Jean-Pierre Kahane (eds), *Fundamental Concepts in Computer Science* (London: Imperial College Press, 2009), p.99.

20 See Edwin Reilly, *Milestones in Computer Science and Information Technology* (Westport, CT: Greenwood Publishing Group, 2003), pp.43ff; Martin Davis, Ron Sigal, and Elaine Weyuker, *Computability, Complexity, and Languages: Fundamentals of Theoretical Computer Science* (Boston: Academic Press, Harcourt, Brace, 1994), p.327.

21 See Henry Hoenigswald and Linda Wiener, *Biological Metaphor and Cladistic Classification: An Interdisciplinary Perspec-*

tive (Philadelphia: University of Pennsylvania Press, 1987). See also Lily Kay, *Who Wrote the Book of Life?: A History of the Genetic Code* (Stanford: Stanford University Press, 2000), pp.2-3.

22 Steve J. Heims, *The Cybernetics Group* (Cambridge, MA: MIT Press, 1991); Lily Kay, "Cybernetics, Information, Life: The Emergence of Scriptural Representations of Heredity", *Configurations* 5:1 (1997), pp.23-91.

23 The prime example in information theory was language – see Claude Shannon and Warren Weaver, *The Mathematical Theory of Communication* (Urbana, Ill.: University of Illinois Press, 1949).

24 Robert O'Hara and Peter Robinson, "Computer-Assisted Methods of Stemmatic Analysis", *Occasional Papers of the Canterbury Tales Project*, 1 (1993).

25 Schlyter's stemma was added in the appendix (ill. 2) of Carl Johan Schlyter and Hans Samuel Collin (eds), *Westgötalagen*, vol. 1 (Stockholm: Häggström, 1827). See also Britta Olrik Frederiksen,'Stemmaet fra 1827 over Västgötalagen – en videnskabshistorisk bedrift og dens mulige forudsætninger', *Arkiv för nordisk filologi*, 124 (2009), pp.129-50.

26 Sebastiano Timpanaro, *La genesi del metodo del Lachmann*, 2nd ed. (Liviana,1981), pp.5-13. Translation by Glenn Most, *The Genesis of Lachmann's Method* (Chicago: University of Chicago Press, 2005).

27 Angelo Poliziano, *Miscellanea* [1489]. For the origins of formal text reconstruction, see Anthony Grafton, *Defenders of the Text* (Cambridge, MA: Harvard University Press, 1991), p.56ff. See also See Glenn Most, 'Quellenforschung', in R. Bod, J. Maat and T. Weststeijn (eds), *The Making of the Humanities, Vol. III: The Modern Humanities* (Amsterdam: Amsterdam University Press, 2014), pp.207-18.

28 See Walter Greg, *The Calculus of Variants: An Essay on Textual Criticism* (Oxford: Oxford University Press, 1927). For an overview, see Vinton Dearing, *Principles and Practice of Textual Analysis* (Berkeley: University of California Press, 1974).

29 For a history of these copying rules in stemmatic philology, see Kari Kraus, 'Conjectural Criticism: Computing Past and

Future Texts', *Digital Humanities Quarterly*, 3:4 (2009), no page numbers.
30 See Willi Hennig, *Phylogenetic Systematics* (Urbana, Ill.: University of Illinois Press, 1966).
31 See Don Cameron, 'Problems in Manuscript Affiliation', in Henry Hoenigswald and Linda F. Wiener, *Biological Metaphor and Cladistic Classification: An Interdisciplinary Perspective* (Philadelphia: University of Pennsylvania Press, 1987), p.302.
32 See Kari Kraus, *ibid.*, 2009. See also Caroline Macé, Philippe Baret, Andrea Bozzi, and Laura Cignoni, (eds), 'The Evolution of Texts: Confronting Stemmatological and Genetical Methods', *Proceedings of the International Workshop held in Louvain-la-Neuve on September 1–2, 2004* (Pisa: Istituti Editoriali e Poligrafici Internazionali, 2006).
33 See N. Platnick and H. Cameron, 'Cladistic methods in textual, linguistic, and phylogenetic analysis', *Systematic Zoology*, 26 (1977), pp.380-85. For an overview of cladistics and other methods in philology, see Macé et al., *ibid.,* 2006.
34 See e.g. N. Cartlidge, 'The Canterbury Tales and cladistics', *Neuphilologische Mitteilungen*, 102 (2001), pp.135-50; Heather Windram, Prue Shaw, Peter Robinson, and Christopher Howe, 'Dante's *Monarchia* as a test case for the use of phylogenetic methods in stemmatic analysis', *Literary and Linguistic Computing*, 23 (2008), pp.443-63.
35 Wilhelm Dilthey, *Einleitung in die Geisteswissenschaften*, pp.29ff.
36 Wilhelm Windelband, *Geschichte und Naturwissenschaft*, 3rd ed. (Heitz, 1904). The discussions by Dilthey and Windelband are more subtle than summarized here. See Bouterse and Karstens, this section ('Focus'), for more details.
37 See Richard Riegelman, *Studying a Study and Testing a Test: How to Read the Medical Evidence* (Philadelphia: Lippincott Williams and Wilkins, 2004). See also Charles Bazerman, *The Informed Writer: Using Sources in the Disciplines* (Boston: Houghton Mifflin, 1995); Lawrence McCrank, *Historical Information Science: An Emerging Unidiscipline* (Medford, N.J., Information Today, 2002).
38 Herodotus, *Histories*, 7.139.

39 Thucydides, *History of the Peloponnesian War*, 1.22.
40 Polybius, *Histories*, 1.1-4.
41 See Bod, *A New History of the Humanities*, 24-26. See also G.E.R. Lloyd, *Disciplines in the Making* (Oxford: Oxford University Press, 2009), pp.67-70.
42 See Kasper Eskildsen, 'Leopold Ranke's Archival Turn: Location and Evidence in Modern Historiography', *Modern Intellectual History*, 5 (2008), pp.425-53. See also Lorraine Daston, 'Objectivity and Impartiality: Epistemic Virtues in the Humanities', in R. Bod, J. Maat, and T. Weststeijn (eds), *The Making of the Humanities, Vol. III: The Modern Humanities* (Amsterdam: Amsterdam University Press, 2014), pp.27-42.
43 Riccardo Fubini, 'Humanism and Truth: Valla Writes against the Donation of Constantine', *Journal of the History of Ideas* 57 (1996), pp.79-86.
44 E.g. Nicholas of Cusa in his *De concordantia catholica*, 1433.
45 For further background on Valla, see Lodi Nauta, 'Lorenzo Valla. Italian Humanist', in *The Classical Tradition: A Guide*, ed. Anthony Grafton, Glenn Most, and Salvatore Settis (Cambridge, MA: Harvard University Press, 2010).
46 For an in-depth biography of Joseph Scaliger and discussion of his works, see Anthony Grafton, *Joseph Scaliger: A Study in the History of Classical Scholarship*, 2 volumes (Oxford: Oxford University Press, 1983-1993).
47 Anthony Grafton, *Joseph Scaliger: A Study in the History of Classical Scholarship*, 2 volumes (Oxford: Oxford University Press, 1983-1993).
48 Joseph Justus Scaliger, *Thesaurus temporum*, Joannem Janssonium, 1658 [1606], p.278.
49 In various places it has been shown that there is a direct line running from Scaliger via Saumaise and Isaac Vossius to Spinoza. See e.g. Jonathan Israel, *Radical Enlightenment* (Oxford: Oxford University Press, 2002), and Eric Jorink, *Reading the Book of Nature in the Dutch Golden Age, 1575-1715* (Leiden: Brill, 2010).
50 See Bod, *A New History of the Humanities*, pp.211-216.
51 Penelope Gouk, 'The Role of Harmonics in the Scientific Revolution', in *The Cambridge History of Western Music*

Theory, ed. Thomas Christensen (Cambridge: Cambridge University Press, 2002), pp.223-45.
52 H. Floris Cohen, 'Music as Science and as Art: The 16th/17th-Century Destruction of Cosmic Harmony', in R. Bod, J. Maat, and T. Weststeijn (eds), *The Making of the Humanities, Vol.1: Early Modern Europe* (Amsterdam: Amsterdam University Press, 2010), pp.59-71.
53 See Rens Bod, *Een Wereld Vol Patronen: De Geschiedenis van Kennis* ["A World of Patterns: The History of Knowledge"] (Amsterdam: Prometheus, 2019), chapter 6. See also Stillman Drake, 'Renaissance Music and Experimental Science', *Journal of the History of Ideas*, 31 (1970), pp.483-500.
54 Stefan Arvidsson, *Aryan Idols: Indo-European Mythology as Ideology and Science* (Chicago: University of Chicago Press, 2006), p.241ff.
55 Martha Nussbaum, *Not for Profit: Why Democracy Needs the Humanities* (Princeton, NJ: Princeton University Press, 2010).
56 See in particular William Bridges, 'A Short History of the Inhumanities', *History of Humanities*, 4:1 (2019), pp.1-26.
57 See Georges Vacher de Lapouge, 'Old and New Aspects of the Aryan Question', *The American Journal of Sociology*, 5:3 (1899), pp.329-46.
58 Noam Chomsky, *Syntactic Structures* (The Hague: Mouton, 1957).
59 Benedikt Löwe, Eric Pacuit, and Sanchit Saraf, 'Identifying the Structure of a Narrative via an Agent-based Logic of Preferences and Beliefs: Formalizations of Episodes from *CSI: Crime Scene Investigation*™', *Proceedings of the Fifth International Workshop on Modelling of Objects, Components and Agents, MOCA'09* (Hamburg: Bibliothek des Dep. Informatik, 2009), pp.45-63.
60 Raymond Williams, *Television: Technology and Cultural Form* (London: Collins, 1974).
61 For such an attempt, see e.g. Rens Bod, *Een Wereld Vol Patronen: De Geschiedenis van Kennis* ["A World of Patterns: The History of Knowledge"] (Amsterdam: Prometheus, 2019), to appear in English in 2021.